Reviews

"Memoirs provide powerful insights into the struggles, challenges and successes of individuals. In so doing, they enhance understanding and strengthen the social fabric of our society. In One Dream: Four Countries, Sundram takes us from his home in Malaysia to Singapore, Scotland and, finally, a life in Australia. With frank honesty he shares his dreams, as well as his determination, despite hardship, to succeed. He does not shy away from revealing familial undercurrents and the impact these had on his life's journey. Sundram highlights the importance of family and belief in oneself. His story underscores the significant contribution new arrivals make to Australian society. An enjoyable read that celebrates the life of one man and provides inspiration for many."
— Helena Bryndzej Studdert, author of *No bed of Roses: Teo's Story*

"Sundram Sivamalai's life and career is one of remarkable determination. In clear lucid prose he tells the story of a young person as green as they come but, nevertheless, endowed with a substance that impels him to turn his dream into a reality. His relentless drive to rise above his impoverished childhood and to further his education sends him across the world. Facing innumerable hurdles at every step of his quest, including his own anxieties and fear, he finds many opportunities that bear fruit. Despite the fire burning in his belly, there is nothing ruthless in his ambition; he displays a selfless compassion and sensitivity to the people he meets as well as a strong commitment to maintain a balance between career and family.

Sundram's inspiring tale of resilience and preparedness to suffer hardship is a model for anyone seeking to rise above their circumstances in the pursuit of their vision.

— Noel Braun, author of *Friend and Philosopher*

"Sivamalai's book, "One Dream Four Countries" is an account of an improbable journey from an impoverished and emotionally deprived childhood in Malaysia, to Singapore, the UK and Australia. The author's determination to obtain higher education and employment comensurate with his qualification is an uplifting story of what that determination can achieve in the face of insurmountable odds. I can guarantee there will be many cultural aspects the reader will not previously encountered or considered."

— Susan Keyssecker, author of *Nobody Chews an Oyster*

"Sundram Sivamalai, from leaving Malaysia & travelling to Singapore at the age of seventeen has experienced at times a difficult, yet opportunistic life as he moved from one country to the other. On many occasions his everyday living was very difficult, but he overcame adversity and took advantage of auspicious moments to improve his everyday life as well as his education, to reach his goals in whatever country he was residing at the time.

Once reaching his last country, Australia, Sundram, now with his wife and family, continued to develop his leadership skills to great advantage.

The story of his life's achievements are inspirational."

— Valerie J. Griffiths, author of *The Coona Girl*

"Sundram, your story, *One Dream – Four Countries* was a wake – up call for me.

I came away from your story with a great admiration for the pursuit of your dream, from abject poverty in Malaysia, taking you on a journey to Scotland and emigration to Australia. Along the way to your dream, all the educational achievements you have gathered in Nursing and Nurse Education, are unbelievable. To add to this, you have gathered a beautiful supportive wife, a son and a daughter who are all successful in their own lives. You could teach us all a few people skills and parenting skills along the way.

The reflections of cultural differences from using a knife and fork to the possibility of your Mum being the victim of Sati when your father died was also something else I have never considered. The "unfair deprivation" you write about for a greater part of humankind has caused me to rethink many of my attitudes to life in general and has made me appreciate this wonderful country even more.

Thank you for choosing Australia as your new home. You have enriched as all with your knowledge, humility and work, and are truly a great example of how to raise good citizens in this country. I hope many people's lives can be enriched by reading your story."

Judith Flitcroft, author of *Walk Back in Time*

One Dream
Four Countries

SUNDRAM SIVAMALAI

Published in Australia by Sid Harta Publishers Pty Ltd,
ABN: 34 632 585 203
17 Coleman Parade, GLEN WAVERLEY VIC 3150 Australia
Telephone: +61 3 9560 9920, Facsimile: +61 3 9545 1742
E-mail: author@sidharta.com.au

First published in Australia 2021
This edition published 2021

Copyright © Sundram Sivamalai 2021

Cover design, typesetting: WorkingType (www.workingtype.com.au)

The right of Sundram Sivamalai to be identified as the Author of the Work has been asserted in accordance with the Copyright, Designs and Patents Act 1988.

The Author of this book accepts all responsibility for the contents and absolves any other person or persons involved in its production from any responsibility or liability where the contents are concerned.

All rights reserved. No part of this publication may be reproduced, stored in a retrieval system, or transmitted, in any form or by any means without the prior written permission of the publisher, nor be otherwise circulated in any form of binding or cover other than that in which it is published and without a similar condition being imposed on the subsequent purchaser.

Sivamalai, Sundram
One Dream — Four Countries
ISBN: 978-1-925707-43-4
pp284

About the Author

Sundram is a Professor of Rural Health with Emotional Well-Being Institute, Geneva, Switzerland. He is invited to sit on several boards. He was awarded the Centenary Medal by the Australian Commonwealth Government for his commitment and support to migrants. He publishes widely on migrant issues in journals and books and speaks at local, national and international conferences on invitation. Sundram and his wife, Subatra, enjoy their time with their son, Dr Anand Sivamalai, who manages his software company in Melbourne and their daughter, Mrs Anuja Seton, with her family in San Francisco (California). Sundram's strong interest, which is to advocate for the culturally and linguistically diverse communities, still continues from his Ballarat (Victoria) residence. He was awarded Ballarat Citizen of the Year in 2021.

Sundram's parents

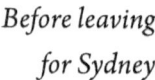

Before leaving for Sydney

Preface

I dedicate the story of my journey to my late parents. I thank them for bearing six children and bringing them up even though they did not live long enough to enjoy their lives with their offspring. I also dedicate my story to all my siblings for their support and care during the "parentless" times in my life. I am grateful to them for their assistance.

Apart from my immediate family, I also thank my relatives and friends who have assisted me in my journey. I am very grateful for the educational support from the Scottish Government that helped me to nurture my career, and I am equally grateful to the Queensland Government and Melbourne University educational support that were undeniably timely in helping me achieve my career goals.

In writing, I reflected on the experiences I had endured, without any influence or coercion from others; as such, those unforgettably sorrowful circumstances that I describe in this book may be uncomfortable to some of my family members. If so, I sincerely apologise to them.

I dedicate this book to my family: my beloved children, son Anand, daughter Anuja, and a special person, my beloved wife Subatra, who stood by me during the challenging times in our life.

Acknowledgement

As the youngest in the family, I am grateful to acknowledge all my siblings for their support and guidance. I acknowledge my second older sister and her family for their "pseudo-parenthood" guardianship during my primary school days of hardship. I will always remain grateful to my oldest brother, an engineer, for his financial support that enabled me to complete my secondary school education. My sincere gratitude to the Scottish Department of Education for the study grant that enabled me to begin my journey into the education world.

Introduction

To share my story has been difficult because I had to "relive" the several uncomfortable moments again when describing past experiences. The main benefit in writing this story has been to allow my long-term unsettled feelings and experiences that were dormant in me to find an outlet to be released, thus settling my emotional wellbeing. During those periods of distressful situations, I had no one to share my circumstances, except with my Lord Ganesha. There were many times I have narrated my sorrows to him that calmed my emotions and gave me the strength to pursue my journey with hope.

In my early years, I realised that I had been deprived the basic privileges that every child should deserve, but, somehow, I was subjected to survive and live in poverty. Such unfair deprivation made me wonder and ask for an acceptable answer as to why I was subjected to such miserable circumstances. Why was I denied my father's love when I was only four years of age and lost him? Then, my mother, who was still alive, was forced to be separated from me also limited the only parental affection that I yearned for at that time when I needed her the most. Why did I not have a "basic house" to grow up in; instead, an infested dilapidated place with poisonous creeping animals that frightened the life out of me daily? Even my daily meals were very uncertain, let alone no proper clothes to cover myself, except for my school uniform, that was reserved for only when I went to school. There were many more unanswered questions to my Lord Ganesha, but with no satisfactory answers. I had to console myself that my birth into such circumstances happened not by choice, but by destiny!

When I realised that there were not many choices left for me to improve my future in that poverty-stricken situation, I had to make a break from it. At the age of seventeen, although I was still very green about the world outside, my desperation forced me to make the brave move. Thus, my journey began, against the tide, as I proceeded to reach my goal.

Contents

Preface	v
Acknowledgement	ix
Introduction	1
1 The uncertainties of leaving my birth country	5
2 Homeless episodes in Singapore	16
3 Lifestyle changes after my father's death	41
4 The great expectations of London	53
5 Embracing Scottish culture	65
6 Surviving Dundee's challenges	81
7 The freedom to make my own decisions	96
8 The unforgettable Hindu wedding	109
9 Unexpected hurdles after my wedding	130
10 Getting what I wanted	146
11 The career plan that went wrong	162
12 My first place to settle in Australia	179
13 Making my first brave move: Brisbane to Sydney	208
14 Embracing the second move: Sydney to Ballarat	234
15 Applying the synergy of community engagements and my career path	250
16 The strategy against my tides	263

‹ 1 ›
The uncertainties of leaving
my birth country

I was wiping my tears and waving to my mother and all my relatives who loved me dearly as the train was about to begin its journey. There were about fifteen people at the Kuala Lumpur (KL) train station platform to see me off. Actually, they were there to convince me not to leave Malaysia. My mother had been crying non-stop for the past two hours as our relatives arrived at the station. I felt very sorry for her, but I was in no position to help her. My uncle (my father's cousin), who was fond of me, was very sad to see me boarding the 10.30 pm train. I had stayed at his house during my school days and had come to know him very closely. Despite me being only fifteen years old when I stayed with him, he had always treated me with marked respect. We were always the last two at the dinner table, dining together over conversations about world affairs.

Seated in the train and looking out, I noticed them pointing to me and crying as the train began to move. I could not control my tears; I had to just let them flow. It was a very difficult moment as I was only seventeen years old and had never been outside of Malaysia.

As the overnight train from KL to Singapore gained speed, I became anxious and mentally unsettled. My mind was full of uncertainties and questions about what my friend might say; would it be, 'I am glad to meet you,' or 'I do not have time for you?'

I realised my mistake of not corresponding with my friend Raja before my journey. The last time we had communicated was six months ago. I wondered whether his friendship towards me might have changed during the four years that I had known him. My seven-hour night journey was so preoccupied with these thoughts that I was restless and didn't close my eyes for a moment.

After the long journey, the train arrived in Singapore at about 5.30am. I was nervous and asked a few passengers seated near me to ensure that I had arrived in the right place, even though I was aware the train terminated there. I carried my suitcase and stepped out of the train onto the station platform. At that moment, I realised how tired my body and legs were due to lack of sleep and my emotional state.

I had meagre savings of RM68 (Malaysian ringgits) that would only enable me to buy food for a few days. That small saving had taken me a few years to accrue through the purchase of 50-cent stamps (100 cents to a Ringgit) during my school days. Each time the book was full of stamps, the total stamp cost was transferred into a post office savings account.

< 1 >   The uncertainties of leaving my birth country

That little money was the only emergency cash I had for the trip.

As I left the Singapore railway station, I felt the coolness of the fresh morning. Singapore has an equatorial climate like Malaysia, so I was used to these cooler mornings that warmed up by midday.

Leaving the train station, I went to catch a bus to Raja's home. Although I was familiar with taking the bus, I was not sure where to wait for it in a different country. As I was unsure of where to stand for the bus, I showed the address to a passer-by, who quickly corrected me to say that I was waiting on the wrong side of the road.

It was not long before the bus stopped and I quickly made my way to a vacant seat in the crowded vehicle. It was just after six in the morning and I noticed there were many uniformed workers, most in heavy-duty work shoes, holding onto their lunch boxes.

I was aware that the public transport in Singapore was no different to Malaysia in that buses did not wait long during passenger pick-ups or drop-offs. As soon as the entering passenger's feet left the ground outside, the bus would accelerate immediately to keep up with the tight time schedule. The only time the bus would come to a complete halt and wait was when the passenger was too frail or had a walking aid. Upon entering the bus, tickets were purchased from the bus conductor who came around as soon as the passengers were seated.

Although it was still dark and appeared quiet outside, the atmosphere in the bus was very lively. From their accents and languages, I recognised several Malaysian immigrants going to work. I had heard from my friends that the manufacturing and ship-building companies in Singapore hired a large number of migrants from Malaysia on temporary work permits. After few weeks, many of their temporary work permits were renewed to long-term work permits, as there was a growing demand for workers. I was watching them and hoping that one day I could be one of those lucky labourers with a job to fend for myself. Before I fell deep into my dream world, I noted that the bus was nearing Jurong, the industrial area of Singapore.

I managed to get off the bus by asking one of the passengers to press the buzzer for the correct stop. I carried my suitcase and showed my piece of paper to the first bystander so that they could direct me to my friend's address.

As I followed the given directions, I was still cursing myself and feeling guilty because I had not corresponded with Raja before turning up unannounced at his doorstep.

I had come to know Raja's family when I followed a friend to visit them at their rice farm during my school holidays. During the few days I was at his house, I followed Raja, who was my age, everywhere he went. After helping him in his rice field, we would cycle to the nearby hawker stalls to eat. We lived in different Malaysian towns 200km apart and had kept in touch when possible, but when I arrived in Singapore, we hadn't spoken in six months.

Several questions began flashing in my mind. *What happens if he does not remember me? What happens if he does not want to help me? Will he see me as a burden and refuse to continue our friendship?*

< 1 >   The uncertainties of leaving my birth country

Before I could think further, I was close to the address and would soon be facing him. I became nervous and realised the gamble that I had taken was not a smart one. It had never even crossed my mind what I would do if Raja was not there or had moved away.

My heart was thumping with anxiety as I climbed the stairs to the correct number on the door of the high-rise building. When I reached the front door, I checked the address again to ensure I was not knocking on the wrong one. I knocked and when the door opened the teenager opening the door looked surprised to see me, especially that early in the morning. She did not wait or say anything when I enquired about my friend; instead she quickly ran off and called for her mother. I introduced myself to the older woman and explained that I was looking for my friend, Raja. She looked at me with a blank expression for a moment and said that he had moved out of the house about six months ago. She also added that she had no idea where he had moved to. From her facial expression it was very clear that she did not want to continue this conversation; she was keen to shut the door and wanted me to take my problem elsewhere. I quickly thanked her and left.

I walked slowly from the building wondering what I would do next. Suddenly, I felt tired and my body was very heavy as I was exhausted. I felt I had completely wasted my time going to Singapore and cursed myself for not having contacted my friend prior to leaving Malaysia. I also wondered why Raja had not forwarded his new address. I felt very angry with myself and questioned why I did not plan my journey better. My

RM68 was just enough for a hotel room if I checked in, but I wouldn't have enough for a meal.

I asked myself if I should I return to Malaysia if I could not find Raja. He was the only reason I had for coming here, and now it would be impossible to find him. I then rationalised that if I was to return, I would be back in the same situation with no job and no income and would end up becoming totally dependent on someone for living without any opportunity to further my studies.

As I stood with these thoughts, I felt helpless and hopeless. I gazed at the myriad tall buildings around me. I thought to myself, *Raja could be in any of those buildings and each of those buildings easily had hundreds of apartments.* I was pondering how on earth I was going to find him in that haystack of apartments? Where or how should I begin the search? I did not know what to do! I was totally absorbed in my own melancholic world of uncertainties and despair.

My excitement about the new place had suddenly changed. I felt lonely and depressed but had no one to share my sorrowful circumstances with. I slowly walked past the hawker stalls with the luggage in my hand to a quiet spot not far from the hawkers.

I was alone in my own world, but the scene around me was very different. In the early morning hours, many of the workers were having breakfast at the roadside hawker stalls before taking the bus to work. There were people calling out yelling to each other and saying goodbye, young smokers in groups having their last draw of smoke before their day began. The scene around me was very erratic, but my own little world was very quiet.

< 1 > The uncertainties of leaving my birth country

I looked up in the sky and called out loud to my father for help. 'Dad, where are you? I've already had enough challenges and I am again totally helpless. I need your help.' I had often said similar prayers in the past when I was desperate and he had rescued me. I hoped he would come again when he heard my call for help.

Although I called for my dad's help, I could only vaguely remember his face; the last time I saw it was at his funeral when I was four years old. That day everyone was crying. I saw my father's body being wrapped in a white cloth; his face left bare. I was being carried around by my uncles and aunts; I knew that something had happened, but did not know that day was the last chance to see my dad's face. That day's sad scenario had stayed with me. I often thought about being in his company and imagined the wonderful experience that could have been for me. My father may have enjoyed four years of my childhood when he was alive, but I could not recall any of my pleasant experiences with him. When I was in school, I had watched children my age with their parents, which brought back memories of my father, whom I missed. My family and the people in the local community had told me that I looked very much like my dad, which I did not believe until I compared his photos with mine. In those photos he appeared to be a very "soft" and kind-looking person.

When things were out of my control and I had no options, I often "asked" him for guidance. That morning in Singapore when I was stranded without a contact to find Raja, I had no choice but to call for his help.

Within moments of my prayer, I saw a young man around

my age crossing the road and heading towards me. I was not sure why, in the early hours of the morning, a stranger was coming towards me. He must have noticed my desperate need for help from my facial expression. He was dressed very casually in a short-sleeved shirt, long pants and a pair of thongs. A bit taller than me, he was smiling and appeared very relaxed as he approached me.

'Are you okay? Did you just arrive?' he asked.

I found his questions sympathetic and not overpowering. His manner was very comforting in my desperate moment. Obviously, it was a great relief that a stranger had appeared out of nowhere and was concerned about my welfare. Before I could answer any of his questions, he guessed correctly that I had just arrived from Malaysia, so all I had to do was simply nod my head and say, 'Yes'. It was quite unusual a shocking experience for a stranger in a crowd to just come up to me and ask if he could be of assistance. Just a few minutes earlier I had seen several strangers pass by me and no one had shown any interest in helping me! People in the community in Malaysia would only come forward to help if you asked for it.

I began to wonder if *this encounter was the work of my dad or* just *a coincidence*. Either way, I thanked my dad who might have helped me in disguise. When the stranger realised I was tired and had just arrived in town, he quickly insisted we have our breakfast together while we continued our conversation. He was very interested to hear about the journey that I had undertaken that morning from Malaysia to Singapore. As we were taking our seats, he yelled out to the nearest hawker to serve breakfast for the two of us. I did not refuse his kind offer

< 1 > The uncertainties of leaving my birth country

to buy my breakfast because I had not eaten anything since my last evening meal in Malaysia, and the smell of the hawker food made me even hungrier.

We sat on the stools at the hawker's stall while our breakfast was being cooked. The "new" stranger began explaining how the job market had attracted many young, unemployed Malaysians to work in the fast-growing shipbuilding industry. He was very upfront in mentioning that many of the Malaysian migrants were from Indian and Chinese backgrounds. As an Indian Malaysian himself, he understood the unemployment challenges for these minority groups. As soon as the breakfast was served, I devoured the *dosai* (Indian pancakes with delicious coconut gravy and chutney), followed by two cups of Indian tea. We washed our fingers and soon left the stall after my stranger paid our breakfast bill.

As we walked, I saw more blocks of tall residential buildings as high as twelve storeys. I asked myself again, *How on earth will I be able to find my friend, Raja, without anyone's help?*

My rescuer noticed my anxiety and suggested that I relax in his apartment while he worked out a strategy to find my friend, Raja. I had no other option but to take his advice as I felt very lethargic and was not able to think clearly, so his suggestion seemed the most appropriate solution. He offered to carry my suitcase and led me into his apartment, his helpful approach reducing my worry. I felt I had a companion and a genuine person who was very understanding of my predicaments and was prepared to help. I assumed again that my prayer to my father had been answered.

As soon as we reached the single bedroom of his company

apartment, I had a shower and changed into something comfortable I had brought along. My rescuer recommended I have a short nap before I stressed myself further. He was absolutely correct that I was very tired, but I could not relax or sleep as my mind was still restless because I had not yet found my friend. My rescuer understood my concern and reassured me that, somehow, he would be found, soon.

While we were exchanging our school experiences, he paused, got up and came back with his Primary 2 class photograph to show me. I was astounded to notice that the class photo he shared was the same as mine. When I looked at it closer, I noticed that in the photograph he was standing three places from me. We were equally amazed. Again, I began to wonder, *Was the unexpected encounter with that stranger a coincidence, or it was help from my dad?* Not sure.

Not long after this, his group of working friends began to drop in at his place, as if he was managing a community hub. I had not known that my rescuer was such a popular person among many of the young temporary workers in Jurong. Obviously, his apartment was used as the main meeting place for several of his friends. My rescuer introduced me to everyone who happened to drop in that day as I repeated the physical description of my friend, Raja, to all of them. I was becoming more hopeful as an active squad of six had started the search, but I could not relax until he was found. It was around 3.30pm that day when one of my rescuer's friends came back and reported to us that he had sighted Raja returning to Block 57 from work.

Around 4.00pm there were several more youngsters

< 1 > The uncertainties of leaving my birth country

dropping in to say that they were also joining the search. By then I knew that the news must have spread and the search must be very active. By 5.00pm, one of my rescuer's acquaintances came back to say that he had spoken to Raja about my arrival and that he had promised to come over to fetch me as soon as he was able to. When I heard the latest news, I was excited and became nervous thinking about how Raja would react upon seeing me. Would he say, 'What made you to come here?' or 'Welcome to the Singapore workers' group?'

After I had heard the comforting message, the clock appeared to go very slowly, and I became more impatient. At around 5.30pm, Raja appeared at my rescuer's apartment with a big grin on his face. I was glad to see he was excited to see me and he gave me a big hug. As Raja was a well-built and very stout person, I was careful that his welcome hug did not hurt me. He sat with my rescuer and me and explained how excited he was to hear of my arrival. At that moment, I felt I was 'saved' as I had finally found my dear friend. While I was calming down, my rescuer and Raja began discussing their work, as that was the first time they had met each other. I was waiting for Raja to finish his conversation so that I could tell him about my journey. Finally, around 6.00pm Raja decided to say goodbye, thanking my rescuer for helping me. On leaving the apartment, Raja insisted on carrying my luggage as we walked to his apartment.

As we were walking, I relayed my journey to Raja, who was amazed to hear about my extraordinary encounter with my classmate. When I noticed how happy Raja seemed with my company, all my anxieties dissipated.

‹ 2 ›

Homeless episodes in Singapore

While heading to his home, Raja was explaining about the difficult accommodation situation in Singapore, particularly for migrant workers without work permits. As I entered his apartment, I was surprised to see his sleeping corner; he had an allocated spot in the single-room apartment to share with four other people. Raja was not a citizen of Singapore and was therefore not entitled to lease any property in his name. Furthermore, he was working as a temporary factory hand and did not qualify for any employer-supported accommodation. The apartment where he was living was officially leased by an Indian worker who had two sons aged nine and ten.

Raja warned me that space in Singapore was limited and finding accommodation was extremely difficult. The rental costs were very high, and properties were much more expensive than in Malaysia. I was lucky that he was extending his hospitality to me.

The one-room apartment was not more than six square

metres and was used as a hall, dining space and sleeping area. Next to the room was a small, two-metre square space that was used as a kitchenette and attached to this was the toilet and shower.

The water from the tap in the bathroom was collected in a plastic bucket for bathing and washing clothes. When I used the bathroom, I was careful not to fully stretch my arms out because there was not enough space.

That evening, after he showed me his apartment, Raja suggested that we leave the premises before the landlord returned from work because he had not yet mentioned my arrival. He was certain that his landlord's two mischievous boys would have loved to give their dad the news about me as soon as he got home. We quickly left my luggage in the room and went for a stroll until late that night, so that when we returned everyone in the apartment would be asleep.

When we opened the door on our return, Raja's landlord was sitting on his bed with crossed legs. When Raja introduced me, his landlord acknowledged me unenthusiastically and agreed that I could stay in his apartment. Raja pointed to my designated sleeping spot, next to his. The sleeping spots were just enough to lie down straight. We had pillows to rest our heads on, a sheet on the floor and another one to cover us, but there was no mattress or other sleeping accessories. As soon as we woke in the morning, we ensured that all our sleeping items were stored away in one corner of the room.

After my arrival, Raja had warned me about his landlord and to keep away from his two naughty boys. He told me that the landlord often returned home drunk after work. Raja told me that every day he returned home around 3.30pm, but would leave the apartment before the landlord returned from work, quietly creeping into the apartment after they were asleep to avoid any conversation with them.

During these evenings out of the house, one of the simple luxuries that we enjoyed was the nearby street markets, where we spent most nights. The street markets sold clothes, food, household items and many other things at reduced rates. In Singapore and Malaysia, the night street markets were alternative forms of shopping. They had become popular with the local residents, particularly those who did not travel to cities for shopping had found them convenient, with competitive prices. The street market in Singapore had more variety of goods for sale than I had seen in Malaysia, with duty-free goods as well. Raja and I took our time to wander the street markets, mainly looking for cheap food and drinks. As I was unemployed, Raja always volunteered to pay for my food and drinks.

When I was a child, soon after my dad's death we had to vacate the comfortable estate house where we were living as we were no longer the family of an estate employee. The large bungalows where we lived were managed by the estate authority. Even our clothes were washed by the *dhobi* (laundry worker) and we did not have to pay. Those majestic bungalows had more than one level with large, spacious rooms that comfortably accommodated the eight members of our family.

With great sadness, we had to move to a rent-free place because we could not afford our rent. The only option we had was my grandfather's dilapidated house. The old house he had built was not at all sturdy looking compared to the estate bungalow. His house had three units, one of which we moved into. A common old unstable veranda attached all three units. The rusted, leaking, tin roof was useless during the heavy monsoon rains as the floors of the rooms got wet. The cement floor had worn out, exposing the clay underneath, with several holes that were ideal for crawling animals. Even during the day, the rooms were dark, but at night we used home-made kerosene lamps to find our way through the house. There was no clean water supply to the house, so we had to fetch water for drinking and cooking from the public tap that was next to the main road about a kilometre away from the house. Water for washing and showers was drawn from the well located at the back of the house about two hundred metres away. We had a wood-fuelled, clay stove at ground level that often took about twenty minutes to get started. The walls and ceilings in the kitchen were covered with soot as there were no windows near the fireplace to let the 'black' smoke escape from the wood fires.

We hardly had any furniture except for an old spring bed with a broken leg. There was an old rattan chair next to the front entrance on the veranda that was seldom used as it was unsafe. In the kitchen there was a bench and an old cupboard that harboured many lizards and mice that ran to hide when they heard our footsteps.

The bathroom next to the main room had rusted tin walls with holes. We had to walk about three hundred metres from the house to use the bucket toilet that was in a small wooden hut with stairs with just enough room to squat over the hole. The bucket at the bottom of the hole was emptied by a privately-paid scavenger who only came at night. As there were no lights in the toilet, we would often find lizards and other creatures in the toilet. There was one very large lizard who always watched me from the ceiling, making me count the seconds until I was out of the toilet.

Generally speaking, the house was not suitable for human habitation, but we had nowhere else to live!

My grandfather's dilapidated house had become a habitat for many creeping animals that often rushed for any leftover food or anything that was left on the table for more than a few minutes. One day, after attending to a visitor at the front door, I came back to finish my coffee and found a dead lizard at the bottom of the mug. That incident made me ask the question how many times the lizards or mice in the house had tasted our food left momentarily unguarded on the table.

Another creature encounter happened one night at about 10.30pm when my sleep was disturbed by an excruciating pain at the back of my neck. I woke my brother up with my cry, and as he lit the kerosene lamp, I got a glimpse of the thirty-centimetre-long, brightly-coloured centipede leaving my mat. The fright of the long, creepy, brownish crawler with so many legs made me cry even louder as it moved away from me.

The house we were in was more home for the creepy crawlies than us, and I felt far from safe. Although my situation in Singapore was less than glamorous, it was a step up from my childhood home.

I often woke up at six in the morning, when Raja was about to leave for work, and planned my activities for the day. My usual routine was to search all the weekly advertised vacancies by 8.00am. By11.30am, I would have written at least five applications. Around 12.30pm, I would go down to the nearest hawker stall and purchase the cheapest lunch, which was usually boiled rice with gravy, for twenty cents.

Following lunch and a short break, I would wait eagerly for the postman. The usual disappointing messages that I received were, something like, 'I regret to inform you that we do not have vacancies ...' or '... sorry to inform you that you were not successful for the position ...'. I was upset by the first few, but soon got used to the negative replies, but never stopped submitting applications.

I found the day passed very quickly, and as the evening approached, I looked forward to Raja's return. Raja noticed that my self-esteem was going down as I had not found any jobs in the first four weeks of my arrival. He often tried to cheer me up and reminded me not to give up. He would encourage me to get out of the apartment to change my depressed state of mind. Sometimes, when I was reluctant to leave, he had to drag me out for a cheap dinner at the hawker stalls. We often carried our packed meals to a public bench to enjoy our food in the open air as we did not have a private place to eat.

About two weeks later, Raja and I were out at the street market for our usual dinner before returning to the apartment around nine at night. We did not know what was waiting for us. Our cheerful mood suddenly vanished as we entered the main building when we heard the noise from our apartment. As we came closer, we saw our landlord's unsteady gait and heard his loud swearing in Tamil that most of the residents in the block would have heard.

His foul comments were directed at us. Earlier that day, his two boys had told their father that Raja had smacked them in the afternoon when they were home from school. That afternoon Raja had had to ask the boys to stop misbehaving but he hadn't laid his hands on them. To get even with Raja, the boys decided to tell their father that Raja had beaten them. When their father returned from work, they must have told him that they had been beaten. Without any discussion or any attempt to find out what had actually transpired that day, the landlord had gone out of control and was yelling and swearing all night.

The landlord knew that we were living in his apartment illegally, and as we were at his mercy, he expected us to live there under his rules. He expected that we 'put up and shut up' with his and his children's bad behaviour. That night, his drunken rage made a horrible scene in the block. Even on normal days, the ground-level traffic noises could be heard, so we were very certain that every resident in the block would have heard his bad language. His noisy behaviour had certainly caught the attention of his immediate neighbours; we saw some of our close neighbours sticking their heads out of their front doors. As the landlord continued yelling, we were both very embarrassed and did not know what to do or how to handle the situation; the only option we had was to leave his apartment immediately.

We had impulsively walked out of the apartment and now that we were outside we realised our sudden homelessness. We could not afford a hotel for the night as I was dependent on Raja for my accommodation and food expenses. We did not know any close friends who could have provided us shelter to sleep for that night. In Singapore, there was, no emergency accommodation and even if there was, we were ineligible to access them as we were there illegally.

So, Raja and I explored all our possible options. We had to get through that night, somehow, but not in his apartment. We thought of the others we knew around the place, but decided not to seek their help because they were also in temporary situations without stable accommodation.

After a quick discussion, both Raja and I decided to leave our packed suitcases with one of the neighbours about three doors away until we found a place to sleep that night.

Suddenly, Raja remembered the "uncle" who lived in the next block of apartments. He had often invited us to watch television at his place. We both quickly ran to his place and explained our situation to him. He expressed his sympathy on hearing our story and kindly offered the T.V. room, the only space in his apartment, for the night. We were both relieved and accepted his offer before rushing back to fetch our suitcases.

As we returned to fetch our suitcases, we were surprised to notice that the neighbours were waiting for us with their doors open. The neighbours, Mrs Rukumani and her husband, Ismail, insisted that we stay the night at their apartment as it was already too late to find accommodation. Furthermore, Mrs Rukumani had been watching our drunken landlord's drama and felt sorry for us. She absolutely did not approve of what had happened to us that evening and the unfair verbal abuse we had received from the drunken man. She had known the two boys were naughty and it did not surprise her. Both Raja and I were very surprised at the offer from a stranger who hardly knew us to take us in for the night. We thanked our "uncle" for his offer and returned to stay with our neighbours for the night.

We both found it very difficult to settle to sleep that night because we could not understand why we were thrown out of the apartment for things we had not done. Regardless, I thanked God for the alternative arrangements we had received in that desperate moment.

I felt very awkward about what had happened to us, even though it was not our fault. I felt that I was partly to blame for the situation we were in. Luckily Raja did not have any "blame" thoughts about me with the incident.

We were lucky that the next day Raja had a day off from work so we were able to discuss our accommodation plans. We enquired at a few places we knew might be suitable, but none of them had immediate vacancies. We both were quite depressed as we did not think that it would be impossible to find temporary accommodation for two young bachelors. We were hesitant to return to Ismail's apartment to share the disappointing news, but around 9.00pm that night, we had to inform them that we needed an extra few days' grace to find an alternative place. We were concerned there was no guarantee we would be able to find one.

Mr Ismail, who had been living in Singapore all his life, was fully aware of the accommodation crisis there. He had discussed our accommodation with his wife and had been waiting for us to come home to share his suggestion.

Ismail wanted to suggest to us that we should stop looking

for accommodation because it would be a waste of time, and impossible to find one within our means. He highlighted that we were both non-citizens of Singapore and did not have work permits, so we would be a liability to any landlord. His suggestions were sound, practical and reasonable. He did not impose any conditions on us to stay with them, only an option to consider. Raja and I were overwhelmed by their generosity and also grateful to them for pointing out to us the reality of our circumstances that we were facing at the time.

After we had accepted their offer to stay with them, we were wondering how on earth we would manage to live with Ismail and his family. As well as his wife and him, there were also two older children, making six adults in the one room that was meant for couples with no children, according to the government allocation.

When we spoke further with Ismail, it became clearer to us how to manage it. He worked night shift and only returned in the morning to sleep, while their first son worked in Malaysia and only occasionally returned over the weekends, staying for a day or two the most. Ismail understood and had worked out the 'changing of the guards' for the sleeping space strategy. During the week, the sleep space was only needed for Raja, me, their second son and his wife, as well as Ismail when he returned in the morning from work.

Ismail was quite strict about our sleeping arrangements. He ensured that we cleared our things from the sleep space when it was not in use. We were all given clear space allocations on the cement floor as to where to place our heads and legs. He expected that as soon as we woke up, all our bedding would be folded and placed in the appropriate spot so that we had enough room to move around. Our stay with the new family in Singapore continued for almost a year; I will never forget their help and support.

After we settled in Ismail's apartment, my life was still very quiet and dull because I had not found a job. I was getting frustrated and hope was fading daily as none of my applications were successful. Initially, I started applying for clerical positions as I met the required advertised selection criteria, but after several rejections I decided I would try for the positions in person rather than through the formal application process. At that time, impromptu interviews were quite common in Singapore. When I turned up for office position interviews, I found that the organisations were quite reluctant to welcome me, which made me feel uncomfortable. As seeking office positions seemed out of the question, I thought about seeking manual labour jobs.

My decision to go for labourer's job was not easy for me, but I was desperate to earn money so that I could survive. One of the reasons I left Malaysia was because, despite being born in Malaysia, I held a red identity card and was not considered a citizen. After my secondary education, I had been teaching in a private school because my Citizenship status prevented me from getting a government job. The income I received from the private school was hardly equivalent to a government school-teacher's salary, but I did not complain because I was hired with no teaching experience for a non-accredited course. Within a couple of months, I was known in the small town 150km away as a 'new, good teacher' and had many requests to conduct private tuition for children in their homes, which supplemented my income.

After eight months of teaching, I heard the shocking news that the principal of the school had left and the school had to be closed. That news crushed my intentions to further my studies because I would soon be unemployed. I also felt sorry for the students and the other teachers who were worse off than me, as they had a family to feed with no social welfare support from the government.

Unexpectedly, I was back to square one with no job and money to survive, but I still had the burning desire to pursue my studies. It was at that time I heard of Singapore, where many young people had gone from Malaysia in search of jobs. I was also corresponding with Raja, who was already in Singapore, so rather than wasting time in Malaysia, I decided to take a chance by going to Singapore.

Given my previous job as a teacher in Malaysia, thinking about a labourer's position was a drastic move, but I was desperate.

Each morning, my job search started with a thirty-minute bus ride, and then walking to every company or factory. It normally took about twenty minutes at each factory or company before I moved on to the next one. I did the same process every day for about a month. I also learned how to gain access to the companies. The security guards at the boom gates questioned you before they would let you through, as if it was a pre-interview. Unfortunately, I had to go through them, otherwise I could not gain access to the company staff.

Mental and physical exhaustion meant I could not continue

the tiring job-seeking exercise past mid-day because the temperature would reach 30°C with around 70 percent humidity, so I would return to the apartment, grabbing the cheapest lunch packet (20 cents) on the way. As that was the first meal for the day, the strong smell of the gravy made me feel like I was starving before I had even opened the apartment door. My biggest treat of the day was lunch. I felt so content with, in fact elated by, that simple food that filled my stomach, and I always thanked God for such a wonderful meal. After lunch, I was too tired to do anything except rest or have a nap for at least half an hour to let the hot and humid afternoon cool down. The afternoon naps, somehow, compensated for those sleepless nights when I remained wide awake worrying about employment.

Following my afternoon nap, I would check the Ismail's old papers for any advertised vacancies that I might have missed. I also made use of the apartment before anyone returned, to bathe and wash my clothes. I would eagerly wait for Raja to return from work. My feelings of loneliness, depression and frustration disappeared the moment I heard Raja turning the door-knob of the front door.

As the days went by, I was getting more frustrated and depressed because I had not found a job. I often asked myself what was blocking me from finding a labourer's job when I was young and fit.

After I had been through 55 companies in person and about 30 unsuccessful written applications, I questioned my approach to the exercise. I thought about the circumstances of a young person who would be desperate for a labourer's position. I realised my education was too high for a labourer, and I had to change my dress code and stop presenting myself so neatly. As my situation was getting desperate, I had to look and behave like a drop-out looking for a manual job.

The very next day I put my new approach into action. My dress code changed from shoes to a pair of thongs, and a short sleeve shirt that hung loose outside my pants. I did not disclose my true qualifications. I was surprised that on the very next day I was able to gain access through the security gates and get into the office to speak to the foreman in the first hour. After he determined that I had dropped out of school after grade six and had no previous work experience, he offered me a job as a sandblaster, starting the very next day. Finally, I had found the secret code!

With excitement, I rushed back to the apartment to share my surprise with Raja, who was very pleased to hear of my new job, although concerned about the kind of job I had accepted. At that moment I had no idea how demanding the job was going to be, but I was determined to feed myself before my finances were completely depleted.

The next day I reported to work well before the starting time and waited for the foreman to arrive. He showed me around the factory and introduced me to an experienced factory hand to be my mentor until I got to know the job. I found that the factory recycled gas cylinders. The empty methane gas cylinders were collected and sandblasted as they were rotated at high speed. The machine sprayed iron filings on the surfaces of empty gas cylinders as they rotated and the old marked labels were removed. Once the labels had been scrubbed off, the cylinders were weighed and freshly sprayed with new labels before they were sent back to the contracted companies.

As a sandblaster, my job was to load the machine on the iron filing spinning machine at regular, continuous intervals. On my first day I found it very hard to lift more than five cylinders continuously to load into the machine. My factory mentor, who was much thinner and appeared weaker than me, showed me how to load the cylinders. For me the job was physically demanding but I had to put up with it because finding another one was not easy.

At the end of my first day, I was physically and mentally exhausted. I asked myself how I had ended up as a labourer like this while others, who had hardly completed their secondary school education, had secured very comfortable jobs with good incomes?

At that time, one thing that kept my spirits high was my belief that one day I would end up with my dream job in health, so I had to face the temporary hurdles.

I was concerned with health and safety conditions of the company. I found the bathroom and toilets for their three hundred workers were not well maintained. They were cleaned only once a day in the morning before the morning tea break but by midday they were stinking. There were no masks provided for the factory workers, even for those who were breathing the black dust of the iron filings like me. Management was aware that when the sandblaster machine was loaded, the dust from the rapidly spinning machine definitely blew into the face of the loader. I covered my nose and mouth with my handkerchief, but was still unable to stop the dust getting into my nostrils and throat. I spent about three minutes every break cleaning my throat before I ate when I was at work. I was concerned about the long-term damage to my lungs from the iron dust inhalation, as I had noticed that young men who had been working at the company for a while were coughing persistently and looked tired most of the time.

That evening I went home and explained about my new job with a bit of forced enthusiasm, but my landlord understood from my facial expressions that I was tolerating it and not enjoying it.

While working as a sandblaster, I explored the possibility of obtaining a work permit to make my position permanent but the Singapore government had very strict guidelines for offering overseas workers permanency. The Government was not keen to employ non-Chinese overseas workers as many companies were owned by Singaporean Chinese; as most of the overseas workers were Malaysians, their rules were very strict.

While I was toiling away as a manual worker, I had not forgotten my dream to obtain a tertiary qualification. One of my main reasons for leaving Malaysia was to seek a university education that would offer me a better life in the future. When I was working as a sandblaster, I often pacified myself by saying that the job was for only a short time and there would be better times ahead. The only way that I knew at that time to break my poverty cycle was to go abroad and explore how to pursue my studies.

I had been in constant correspondence with my oldest brother, Krishnan (Krish), who was already in Dundee, Scotland. He had left for the United Kingdom (UK) two years before I came to Singapore. He pursued his studies using his savings from working as a technician in Malaysia. I had no savings so I couldn't fund my own studies. But, had I explored the option of studying abroad, I would have found there were opportunities abroad to do nursing for a minimal wage and also with a qualification at the end of it.

The idea of studying further was constantly at the back of my mind. Although I was managing in Singapore, the thoughts about my study ambitions were making me restless. The income from my tiring work was not enough to put myself through education in Singapore. Furthermore, I would not be able to manage my studies after finishing the physically demanding work all day. While I was very grateful to Ismail for his hospitality, his apartment hardly had space for a chair or table for me to study at.

I often dreamt of leaving the miserable life I was facing in Singapore and looked forward to the day when I had a decent place to sleep, normal food to eat and the nice clothes I always dreamt of. I was yearning to escape from my terrible situation. When I discussed my idea with Raja, he always encouraged me to chase my dreams.

When Krish agreed that I should do nursing, I knew that my family would also be happy, because if I moved closer to him in the UK I would be under his guidance. Soon after Krish's endorsement, I submitted several applications to England to study nursing, but he wanted me to apply for a place in one of the nursing schools in Dundee, as he was studying at the university there.

I felt good about myself and was much happier because

< 2 > Homeless episodes in Singapore

I was dreaming that my future would be much better if and when I went overseas. I began to concentrate more at work. My sleep was better and my self-esteem improved as I was already in a dream world. I shared my excitement with only a few friends, but soon the news about my overseas trip spread to nearly all my acquaintances as well.

Even though I had not received any confirmation of a place in nursing from any of the schools, my excitement was building up daily. Some nights I found it hard to sleep because I was already imagining that I was there. Although I was very positive about going overseas, some of the stories I had heard made me nervous. Several of the boys who had gone overseas to further their studies had not returned home upon completion of their courses, while others did not even finish their studies. Some of the disappointed parents, who had borrowed money from relatives and friends to send their children abroad to study, had to pay off the debts themselves with great grief. When I remembered such incidents, I was worried what might happen if I did not succeed in my studies and ended up like one of those boys. I had created a high expectation amongst my family and friends that I had to honour.

One day I received a letter that changed my life forever. That was the offer note from Ninewells College of Nursing and Midwifery in Dundee, Scotland. I was thrilled to read the news and thanked God and my father in Heaven for providing me a chance to embark on the path I had been dreaming about for the past few years. I shared my great news with Ismail and Raja, who were equally happy for me.

Although I was excited about going abroad, the thought about the costs really hit me. I was not sure how I would prepare myself for the expense of getting there. I proceeded to prepare for the journey with what I could financially manage. Getting some new clothes was number one priority for me as I hardly had any proper clothes to wear. Fortunately, Ismail had lived in Singapore for a long time and knew the local tailors very well, and it was with his connections I got my clothes at a very reasonable rate. I chose different coloured shirts with a mixture of different materials, but cotton was my favourite. I was excited to purchase new clothes because that was the first time in my life I was able to afford them, and not a single one was white.

During my school days I did not have any decent clothes to wear, except my white school uniform. Every year, I received a pair of new clothes for the Hindu festival of Deepavali. Those clothes were always white because after I had worn them on the festival day, they became my school uniform, so my mum did not have to buy two lots of clothes. She also bought clothes that were slightly too large so that I would not outgrow them before the next twelve months were over.

I often admired my privileged classmates who wore coloured clothes for physical activities in the afternoons. Their coloured sports shorts looked very smart with their T-shirts and matching shoes. Meanwhile, my attire was the same white shorts and top that I had worn to school that morning because I had no other clothes. When I noticed my classmates, I often dreamt how smart I would look if I could afford to wear something that was not white. Buying my new clothes in Singapore, I finally started to feel I was reaching my dreams.

I also purchased a winter jumper as I was aware that the weather in Scotland was cold right through to summer. I purchased a luggage bag, a pair of leather boots, a wrist watch and pair of sunglasses. They were comfortably packed in my new luggage bag and weighed under 25kgs, well under the allowed luggage weight of 31kgs.

As I was returning with Ismail from the last day of my shopping spree, I was worried about the cost of the airfare which I had not budgeted for. Luckily, the very next day I received a note from my brother Krish saying that he would purchase the one-way ticket to Scotland. He said I had to organise all the travel documents and be ready to depart for Scotland within a month. Upon reading that message I became more anxious with excitement as I knew that I was really leaving Singapore. I had a very short time to prepare for the journey and my visa application had to be done through the Malaysian government, who also had to provide a sponsorship letter before the UK visa could be finalised.

I had to leave Singapore well ahead of time to return to Malaysia to organise all the travel documents and say goodbye to my brothers, sisters, mother and close relatives. I knew my aged relatives had to be informed of any events of a significant nature, and leaving the country was considered one, not to mention that many of my extended family were very fond of me and they were interested in being included in my goodbye rounds.

As planned, I tendered in my resignation at work and concentrated on my departure preparations. The friends at work, who had come to know me very well, were happy for me to pursue my career path. My supervisors at work were sad to lose me as I was a 'good worker' but also wished me well for my future endeavours. The search party youngsters, who had helped me in locating Raja when I first arrived in Singapore, were happy for me and they all wished me the very best of luck before my departure from Singapore.

I was very sad to leave Ismail and his family, and my friend Raja. I told Ismail that I would always remember him for the help and advice he offered me during my difficult times. Raja, as usual, 'cracked' some jokes during those emotional moments to lighten things up. It was incredibly difficult to say goodbye to him after all the help he had offered me.

All of us were in tears when I boarded the train to return to Malaysia. I sat still for most of the journey, with fond memories of Singapore and the good friends I was leaving behind. As the journey continued, I fell asleep and I was soon looking forward to disembarking at Kuala Lumpur. By the time I reached my destination, the information about my arrival had spread to my relatives who were all expecting to see me before I left for the UK.

After my arrival in Malaysia, I had to prepare my travel documents, but had no idea where to begin or how I should start the application process. The first thing I did was to go to a travel agent, as advised by one of my friends, with all the essential travel details and my personal documents.

As I had not travelled overseas before, I did not understand the flight protocols or the visa requirements needed for entry into foreign countries. My travel agent knew almost every legal requirement for entry to the UK so he prepared the necessary travel documents prior to booking my ticket. Unfortunately, my visa application did not get approved on time so my travel was delayed by a few months. I had a stressful time, waiting with my bag packed for the journey. Eventually my visa approval came through, four months later. I was so glad to go to the British Embassy in Kuala Lumpur (KL) for the sixth and final time to get my passport stamped so that I could enter the UK.

I had watched movies with melancholic departure scenes, but did not experience such feelings until I had to say goodbye to my loved ones. Waiting at the airport, my heart became heavy, my mouth dried up and tears welled in my eyes; I was lost for words.

Several of my relatives who lived close to the international airport in Kuala Lumpur were there to farewell me. I had requested families with no transport not to feel obligated to come, but they were at the airport with their children after finding their own way there. There were around thirty of them in small groups, busy in conversation with each other.

My second oldest brother, Subramaniam (Maniam), was not there as he was posted to East Malaysia with the Malaysian Territorial Army at the time of my departure, but he had already conveyed his farewell to me.

My third older brother, Manoharan (Mano), was already in a very emotional state; he was concerned as he had heard many boys who had gone overseas for higher education had settled in foreign countries and not returned.

My oldest sister, Saraswathy (Saras) who was very fond of me, had already expressed her apology that she would not be there with her seven children as most of them were of school age. But she ensured that her husband and eldest son would be there to farewell me.

My second older sister, Jayaletchumy (Jaya), who lived 200km from the airport, had arrived near Kuala Lumpur a day earlier via public transport. On the day of my departure, she, together with her husband and children, were at the airport. She was also very fond of me as I was her youngest sibling and had lived under her family's care for several years during primary school.

All my siblings were delighted that I had the opportunity to leave the country for a better future, but they were sad to say goodbye to me.

My mother was already teary and began crying as the time approached for me to say goodbye to her.

She said, 'I lost one son to the army,' referring to Maniam, who had hardly been with her since enlisting.

'My first son left the country for good,' she said, referring to my brother, Krish, whom I would be meeting in a few hours in London. He had left four years ago and showed no signs of returning, although he had promised my mother he would return within three years. I could understand my mother's perspective as she had been a widow since I was four years old and seeing her children leaving the country would have been heartbreaking for her. She was unable to control her emotions and her sobbing was getting louder and louder by the minute. The most difficult thing in the world for my mother was to let go of me at the airport.

She said, 'I will be dead before you return.'

By now I was sobbing too; and finally, Maniam had to drag her away from me so that I could proceed to customs before boarding the plane. By the time I left my mother, we had certainly caught the attention of everyone at the airport with my departure scene.

I was wiping my tears as I passed the checkpoint into the customs area and was uncomfortable passing through customs. I had to ask the officials for assistance with my paperwork as I was quite anxious, but I was not shy in asking people for help to make sure that I was doing the right thing. I noticed other passengers were relaxed and enjoying their walk towards the boarding lounge, whereas I was too nervous in the large, open environment as I was brought up in a small town and not used to so many strangers in a strange new environment.

I saw many passengers who were comfortable in their suits, whereas I felt very uneasy in mine because it was my first time wearing one. I felt the tie was restricting my neck as if it were a rope.

Finally, I reached the gate next to the boarding lounge at least sixty minutes before the scheduled boarding time and saw many of the passengers already waiting with their hand luggage. I did not sit for long before I had to go to the toilet. I had never seen a urinal before and I didn't know how to work it, so I waited and watched the next user to copy his actions.

I returned to my seat still feeling very uptight, noticing many passengers reading papers or books while relaxing, unlike me. I kept looking at my watch every few minutes so that I did not miss the plane, not realising that everyone sitting in the lounge would be boarding the same flight. The large pre-departure lounge was filling up as the boarding time was getting closer. I was telling myself to calm down and relax, but it was not that easy.

As soon as I felt that I could not do anything else except wait, I began to feel very lonely. I was already missing my family, whom I had left about an hour ago. I felt helpless and uncertain about the journey I was about to undertake.

When the announcement was made for passengers to come through the boarding gate, I just followed the crowd. I was glad to notice that my boarding pass looked the same as everyone else's.

As I followed the crowd and walked into the plane, I realised how spacious it was inside. My suitcase had been checked in before boarding, so my hands were free as I walked in. I took my seat as directed by the flight stewardess. I was unsure on how to buckle my seat belt, so I waited and copied the actions of one of the passengers seated across from me.

As all the passengers were seated, I looked out of my plane window and was surprised to see my mother, brother and sister standing on the viewing deck, waiting for the plane to take off. I could make out that my mother was being consoled by my brother. I saw her arms and body moving non-stop, pointing to the plane that I was in. I assumed that she was still crying because I was leaving. As I watched her from my seat, it brought tears to my eyes. I waved to them from my seat, not knowing that they would not be able to see me. I had been waiting for years for this moment, but having said goodbye, I suddenly felt very uncomfortable.

‹ 3 ›
Lifestyle changes after my father's death

As I was waiting for the plane to be airborne, thoughts of my mother saddened me. She had lost her husband in her early thirties and now her children were leaving her.

My father's death brought about a swift change in my mum's lifestyle as she had no support from anyone, not even my father's siblings. The only reason she had come to Malaysia from South India was because of my father, whom she had married in an arranged wedding at the age of thirteen.

She was the only girl in her family, with three older brothers who loved her dearly. I remember my mum speaking to me about her family members with great affection and positive wonderful moments of fun with her brothers in her home village. Although her family was not rich, she cherished the fond memories of love given by them. Adjusting to being a young bride without her family around would have been a great challenge, especially so young. Leaving her South Indian Tamil culture behind and moving to the "new" cosmopolitan Malaysian culture, must have been incredibly stressful.

She often described herself as belonging to a superior caste. The amenities in her caste-bound village in India were solely for the use of the people of similar caste and others were forbidden from using them. For my mother, learning to live in a different environment, which was caste-free but culturally diverse, must have been very difficult.

The sudden death of my father made my mother very unsure on how to manage her six children alone. Although my father's relatives knew of her challenging circumstances, they did not offer any help or moral support during my mother's dire times. The only person who was always ready to support her was her father-in-law, my grandfather.

Without any income for house expenses, my mother had to draw the money from my father's drying-up death insurances. She knew that she had to find work, but was unsure how because she had not worked when my father was alive. Her cultural village life in India did not encourage the education of women and therefore she had not been to school nor had any work experience. She was not able to read or write, even in her mother tongue, and was unable to converse in Malay (the national language of Malaysia).

In addition to the financial challenges, her caste system had implications on her life as a widow. Fortunately, she escaped the practice of *sati* as she was in Malaysia at the time of my father's death; in the traditional Hindu practice of *sati*, the widow had to end her life on her husband's funeral pyre to prove her love and devotion to her husband. Her caste system also forbade widows partaking in auspicious Hindu celebrations because of the belief that they would bring bad luck, so my mum avoided attending many celebrations. The caste system also expected Hindu widows to wear a white sari, without any jewellery or flowers in their hair. The rationale for such a dress code for widows was not to look beautiful because that might attract other men.

Luckily, my mum did not practise *sati* because all six of us would have become orphans, but she did have to wear a white sari. As I grew older, I realised the Indian caste system focused more on how the community perceived widows negatively rather than helping the individuals and their families. I was amazed at how she had managed to survive all by herself in the unfair, male-dominated caste system predominantly practised by Indians in Malaysia.

Through her determination, my mother managed to raise us without a husband, which was an amazing achievement. The pain and suffering to nurture her six children between the ages of four to seventeen in a "man's world" was unthinkable in that era.

Given our living conditions, my primary school years were stressful times because I did not have the basics that a school-going child needed. I was grateful for the support of my siblings, who offered whatever they could within their means, because we were all in the same situation. As a child, there was no love or caring for me at home. Throughout my primary school years, I was moved around to live with my siblings; I was moved around from my oldest brother (Krish) to my second older sister (Jaya) and back to live with my grandfather, who was in his sixties by then. Moving me around to different towns disrupted my schooling, but was inevitable as everyone lived in different parts of Malaysia. They also probably didn't think I would continue schooling beyond primary school, so my survival and care were their top priority, not my education.

I can remember going to school and coming home as a chore because I had to walk 6km every morning to school. I had to leave the house early for the one-hour journey by foot to be there by 7.00am. When school was over at 1.00pm, I walked home in the hot and humid weather, very tired, and looked forward to eating whatever was left over from the previous night's dinner.

Then there was an interesting unexpected episode that happened because of my clothes limitation.

When I was in Primary 4, at the age of ten, the Methodist school I attended had a very strict school uniform policy. The boys were only allowed to wear short-sleeved shirts, shorts, socks and shoes, all in white. Given my circumstances, I had only one decent, wearable uniform that I often washed after school and wore the next day. My uniform was wearing through quickly because it was being washed three times a week. One morning, I discovered a big tear at the back of my shirt just before going to school, my mother tried desperately to purchase a white shirt from the provision store where we usually bought things on credit, but unfortunately, they had no white-collared shirts, only white T-shirts. I saw my mother's disappointment that morning when she had to console me into wearing a white T-shirt that was usually worn under the shirt. Understanding her circumstances,

< 3 > Lifestyle changes after my father's death

I quietly accepted wearing it to school that morning. As I walked through the small town to school, I was looking at every passer-by to see if anyone was watching me as I felt very uncomfortable.

That whole day at school I felt half-dressed and was very embarrassed to mix with my classmates. I was very quiet in class and refrained from socialising because I was conscious of my odd T-shirt.

I could not wait to remove my shirt as soon as I got home. I was relieved to notice that my mother had managed to purchase an appropriate collared shirt to wear to school the next day. When I reached school the next day, I noticed that there were seven other boys who had come to school with T-shirts. I was puzzled that they had copied my style, but I was surprised that I had caused such a sudden fashion trend in my school. The T-shirts that those boys were wearing were silk and much more expensive than my cotton shirt had been. Their shirts were tailor-made and better fitting and therefore had a "cool plus" look about them. From that day onwards the school policy changed, allowing boys to wear white T-shirts because it did not violate the school uniform policy.

One of the concerns my mother had faced following my father's death was managing all six of us. The two oldest children in our family were girls. In my family, like any other Indian households, the parents would prefer their daughters to marry before they reach the age of nineteen, but my mother preferred they were married by their eighteenth birthday.

Marriages are usually a costly business and my mother was not in a financial position to offer dowry payments to the grooms. Fortunately, during my father's hospitalisation he had discussed my older sisters' marriages with my mother.

My sisters' prospective grooms had very different personalities. My oldest sister, Saras (Saraswarthy), named after the goddess of knowledge, was married to a reliable man of the same caste, related closely to my mother's family in India. He was the only son and breadwinner for his parents, whom he lived with in Malaysia, and his sister, who lived in India. His parents were in their fifties, but maintained their farm of forty cows, fifty goats, forty chickens, eight dogs and three cats. They had their own private generators and large tanks of rainwater for drinking and cooking. They lived five hundred metres away from the nearest town and therefore seldom went shopping.

Saras' would-be husband was a well-educated Indian scholar who lived and worked as a mechanic for a tin-dredging company in Malaysia. He was a very task-orientated person and seldom found time to socialise. After his primary work in the day was over, he was away at his second job till evening.

My mother agreed for Saras to be married to him, but was concerned about the daily chores and the lack of support at home for my sister. My brother-in-law was keen to help her with the house chores, but was away most of the time with his second job. Despite these reservations, my mother still got her married to him.

Not long after my oldest sister's wedding, my second sister was married to the man my dad had discussed with my mother. My second older sister, Jaya (Jayaletchumy), named after the goddess of wealth, was more talkative and very forward.

< 3 > Lifestyle changes after my father's death

She would not hesitate to question someone if she did not understand them. Such assertive behaviour was not accepted in many traditional Hindu families.

Jaya's husband was quite different to Saras'. He was of Indian origin, but had no family living with him. He had a younger brother and an uncle he seldom saw. He had followed his uncle (his mother's brother) who had migrated from India in search of a better life and came to know my family when my father was alive. His honesty and straightforwardness earned him my father's respect. His slim and well-built figure matched Jaya's beauty. He had completed primary six in Tamil and had been in the Army Reserve. As he was living by himself, he visited our family during his days off from work. My father knew he had become fond of my sister. When my father was paralysed after his accident, he advised my mother to get Jaya married to this man. My mother also liked him because he was from the same caste, with a pleasant caring personality.

Soon after the weddings, my two older sisters had to leave us and move in with their husbands, leaving the remaining boys (all four of us) living with my mother.

My mother's financial position was not good after losing her husband. She was constantly finding ways to bring in some cash while keeping the housing costs to a minimum. The lack of food, poor living conditions and no income had created ongoing tensions in our household. I nervously witnessed the small quarrels between the siblings that escalated into very harsh words and ended in physical violence.

House chores were the other reasons for the tensions in the family. One challenging chore was fetching drinking water from the public roadside tap a kilometre away. Although I was too young (seven years old) for that chore, I still helped to fetch water, carrying two buckets (between 12 and 36 litres). Although we often bathed and washed clothes at the well that was only two hundred metres away at the back of the house, we still had to carry water home for other use. Gathering firewood for cooking was not anyone's favourite job, but it had to be done.

My mother was desperately searching for work, but was not successful. I was not surprised at her difficulty finding work because she was illiterate, unable to converse in the local Malay language and had no work experience. After several failed attempts, she decided to cook deep-fried Indian savouries to generate some income. She was helpless and very concerned about our welfare as our next meals were not very certain. I had observed my mother on many occasions foregoing her meals when there was not enough for all of us to eat. Often, she refrained from eating or pretended to be full and only ate the leftovers, if there were any.

The tension in the house was escalating by the day as my oldest brother, Krish was becoming more dominant and began controlling everyone. At that time, he was eighteen years old, but did not comprehend my mum's desperate situation. As he was short-tempered, he yelled at us (his three younger brothers) and on many occasions smacked us, although often mum came to our rescue. One day, the tension between my mother and Krish, was unbearable and my brother ordered my mother, who was very nervous and frightened of him, to leave the house.

< 3 >   Lifestyle changes after my father's death

At that time, my mother did not have any choice and was unable to defend herself. Depressed and frightened, she left the house with her few clothes in a plastic bag. I was petrified and nervously watched my helpless mother finally leaving. The next day the house felt different and the little support I had felt in the house slipped even further. I was sure that all of us were missing her, and I was certain my oldest brother, who was responsible for what had happened, felt remorse for what he had done. Being the youngest, I missed her terribly.

As he was a student, Krish had a difficult time managing study and part-time work. Every morning he had to cycle for thirty minutes, followed by a forty-five-minute bus journey, to attend his secondary education in the next city, as our small town's schools stopped at lower secondary level. Fortunately, the rest of us had not reached secondary education and did not have to leave town every morning, but we had that daily six-kilometre walk.

I was upset with the poor financial situation that we were facing. Even our basic meals became difficult. I had to hunt for green edible plants or vegetables in the wild for our next meal. My two oldest brothers, Krish and Maniam, began searching for weekend work, as we were all attending classes during the week. They were aware that they did not have any work experience and finding work that was only on the weekends, was not easy. After several visits to a nearby estate, the contractor there decided to hire them for labouring work on weekends. The hard labour of spraying weedkillers in a rubber plantation was physically demanding and the chemical they were handling was dangerous. They had to fetch water from a distant creek in buckets to dilute the toxic weedkillers before spraying them. Furthermore, the weeds were thick and infested with poisonous tropical reptiles. The small wages for such a hazardous job was not worth the risk, but there was no other alternative.

Those days were not easy for them, working weekend jobs and managing their studies while looking after their two younger brothers. Somehow, we managed to make it through our tough period, all while managing the house, continuing our studies and paying our expenses.

It was quite surprising how my two oldest brothers, who worked together to earn money for our survival, had different personalities. Maniam was not as ambitious or domineering as Krish. Maniam was a sensitive person who listened to my concerns; his calm and relaxed approach was comforting and I enjoyed sharing my views with him. Krish seldom had time to listen to anyone's views; he had established his authoritative position within the family circle since my father had passed away.

The personality differences and the economically challenging circumstances at home caused inevitable squabbles between the two older brothers, which had become common. The culmination of our poor living conditions, lack of food, poor indoor lighting, poor bedding and no drinking water escalated the tension between them. I became petrified and shed tears helplessly watching the intensified arguments that sometimes ended in physical violence.

I felt sorry for my brother, Maniam, as it was difficult for him to concentrate on his studies under Krish's domineering

< 3 > Lifestyle changes after my father's death

attitude. Krish expected to control his younger brother and failed, and eventually Maniam left the house.

For me, it was another big loss. He was the only older brother with whom I was able to communicate without fear. He had allowed me to speak my mind, even if I disagreed with his view. When Maniam left the house, I became even more terrified and I had no one to comfort me.

Krish's strict disciplining of me was wasted at times. I remember he forced me to get up by 5.00am to do my school reading, as he believed the morning was the best part of the day for learning. To me that was an utter waste of time because I was only eight years old and I needed eight hours sleep to "recharge my body battery". Unfortunately, I did not have any choice but to obey him, otherwise I would get further slaps. After the wasted hour in the morning, I had to rush my six-kilometre walk to school and by the time I got to school, I was often tired and sleepy.

When I reached home, I ate the leftover food from the previous meal for my lunch and had a bit of relaxation time until Krish returned in the evening. Before he got home from work, I had to help in preparing the evening meals, do my homework, clean the house and finish my washing. My third brother, Mano, who was also living with us, seldom helped me with the housework or supported me as a brother.

Mano, three years older than me, was of a very different character. On one occasion, he had spent his school fees on himself and his friends instead of giving it to the school. He had been absent from school without reason and his performance at school was poor. During school days he often came home late after seeing his friends on the way. Sometimes, when our concerned relatives advised him of his unacceptable behaviour, he abruptly reminded them to mind their own business.

So, my life was not happy at all. I was missing my mother and living under the fear of my oldest brother. I could not predict when he would become angry. During those days, going to school was my escape, but my anxiety levels would increase again by the evening when I returned home because of Krish.

Sometimes I thought about the reasons for my brother Krish's domineering behaviour. It could have been because of the responsibilities he took on at seventeen years to look after his three (Maniam, Mano and me) brothers. He cared for our education and sheltered us, but denied us the love we needed at the time. He supported and guided us but did not comfort us, instead induced fear. As he was young himself and had no life experience, I have to forgive him because he did what he assumed was best for our welfare.

So, the loss of my father not only affected my mother, but our entire family's life. In leaving Malaysia, I hoped to create a better life by leaving my sadness behind.

‹ 4 ›

The great expectations of London

The cabin doors closed and I heard the captain's announcement to fasten our seat belts as the plane began moving. Soon the plane was increasing speed, I felt a bit nervous and closed my eyes as the plane tilted before it was airborne.

I do not remember anything after that until I was woken by the air hostess for a drink. I had no idea about what drink I should have. I had heard that some passengers used strong alcoholic drinks to fall asleep during flights, but as I had no experience with alcohol, I chose a soft drink. I was beginning to enjoy the in-air experience and the clean air in the plane.

I observed that 80 percent of the people in the plane did not look the same as the people I often encountered in Malaysia. I admired their elegant clothes. When the seat belt signs turned off, many of the smartly-dressed children who had been quiet suddenly became mobile. I watched the children moving; walking up and down the aisles while their parents were busy talking to each other and drinking alcohol. They were happy to be left alone and entertained themselves. I observed several older children remain in their seats while playing with toys. Some of the passengers seated near me were quietly engrossed in their books, while I was like an alien who had fallen from the sky into the plane, watching all those activities with great excitement.

I overheard two European women speaking in English, but I was only able to understand some of the words. I felt frustrated for not quite understanding the conversation. I then realised that the English spoken by the Europeans was different to Malaysian English.

As soon as the dinner announcement was made, I quickly dashed to the toilet. Luckily, it was similar to the one at the airport. I was fine until I was about to leave the toilet and flush it. The suction that followed the "whoosh" noise made me jump. I thanked God that I did not have to pick up anything from the toilet bowl because if I had to, I would have been sucked into the flush!

As soon I was seated, my dinner was served. The food on the tray looked very different to the Malaysian dishes I was used to. I noticed that there was a fork and spoon on the tray which I had no experience with. Eating my dinner with this cutlery was going to be a challenge.

All my life I had used my fingers to eat, as per the traditional Indian practice. In many of Indian restaurants and homes in Malaysia, food was served on banana leaves and eaten with fingers. Malaysians from non-Indian origins, such as the Malays and Chinese, had also learned to eat Indian food with their fingers. I had comfortably learned how to eat with chopsticks. In this plane, my only choice was to use the cutlery. I waited and watched how others were managing their food with the cutlery before I started using it. It took me a long time to feed myself, but I managed it!

I found the experience very different, and the British cuisine bland and dry. There was none of the usual rice and spicy gravy to mix the food with. Although the cuisine was quite strange to my palate, I knew I had to get used to it because I would be eating similar dishes in the future. Throughout the flight I continued eating all the food that was served because I had nothing else to do.

I was enjoying the comforts of the plane, but there was not much to see through the windows except the passing clouds. The temperature in the plane was ideal to sleep in, and they even provided a blanket. It did not take long before I stretched myself out into the two empty seats next to me. I was glad to leave the hot, humid and uncomfortable temperature of Malaysia behind and to enjoy the ideal climate in the plane. Soon I could not control my eyes, dozing off until I was woken by new noises.

I suspected it was breakfast time because I heard the stewardess wishing passengers a good morning. Cornflakes with fresh milk, bread rolls, coffee and fruits were being served. That was the first time I had seen cornflakes in my life! Again, I watched how others ate before I began eating mine. After my first mouthful I found it terrible and not tasty at all. Luckily, I managed the bread with butter and marmalade without any worries, and I was pleased to see the local fresh fruits on my plate which I was familiar with.

After breakfast, I was feeling comfortable and dreamt of my destination. I had read about the cold Scottish climate and seen pictures of people dressed in warm clothes most of the time. I also wondered how I would adjust to the new environment and cope with the cold weather and European culture.

My optimistic dreams quickly vanished when I remembered my brother Krish was going to be my guardian in London. I prayed that I wouldn't re-experience the same treatment I had during my primary school days. I knew my flight would soon end and I would be in London facing him after several years. At that time, I was in my twenties, whereas he was in his thirties and I hoped he would not treat me like a child. I expected some dignity and respect and no more domineering behaviour. I soon fell asleep again.

My dreams were interrupted when I heard the captain announce the crew should prepare for landing. When I checked the local time, it was 3.00pm. I looked out of my window and saw the picturesque tall buildings with their lights on. I had not seen such tall buildings before. As the plane touched down on the runway, it was not as bright as Malaysia or Singapore. The sun had almost disappeared and all of the airport buildings were brightly lit. I remembered that it was towards the end of autumn and the beginning of winter, so the sun was setting early. While the plane was slowing down, many passengers were putting on their thick jumpers and cardigans to prepare for the cold. Luckily, I was wearing my suit, but did not have any extra warm clothes with me. The few woollen clothes I had purchased were in the luggage I would collect after the flight.

< 4 > The great expectations of London

The eighteen-hour flight was tiring even with interrupted sleep, and my body was sensitive to the sudden cold.

As I was leaving the plane, I looked outside and had a shock to see so many people at the airport, far more than I had seen in Kuala Lumpur. Many of the people I saw looked very different to the ones I was used to in Malaysia or Singapore. There were a few who looked Chinese, and others with darker skin, who I assumed might be from the African continent.

Several of them were wearing some kind of head cover. I was not sure whether it was for the cold season or cultural reason. Many of the men had plain-looking hats whilst the women had very colourful furry hats. Many of them were wearing leather shoes that covered up to their ankles. Nearly all of them had gloves to cover their hands, and scarves over their necks and chest.

It took approximately two hours after landing for me to walk through Heathrow Airport and out of the surveillance area. The coloured lanes guided me to the immigration counter within forty minutes, and in another thirty minutes I was at the carousel to collect my luggage. The final thirty minutes was spent at customs, and within minutes I was on the "nothing to declare" exit lane. As I came out, I spotted my brother who was waving to me with a grin. He was emotional and delighted to see me. I noticed his teary eyes; I was happy to see him, but at the same time not quite sure what was waiting for me.

I was very grateful that he had helped me to get to the UK but the thought of staying under his control made me feel very uncomfortable. He enquired about the family in Malaysia and how everyone was keeping. As we walked, he insisted on carrying my luggage for me. He looked tired as he had come directly from work to fetch me during busy hours in London. When I arrived, he was a full-time Engineering student at Dundee University (Scotland), but worked part-time during his semester breaks in London (England). He needed work during his holidays to pay his university fees as his savings were shrinking.

We managed to take a taxi from Heathrow Airport to Kings Cross Station and continued the journey by bus to his residence in Colindale, a suburb of London. The taxi that we took did not look the same as the ones in Malaysia; it was spacious with a separate compartment between the driver's seat and passengers' seats. I presumed the communication between the passenger and the driver was through a sliding glass window for security reasons. The two rows of seats in the back of the taxi had the capacity for six passengers to be seated comfortably, with ample space for luggage.

From the airport to the train station I was looking outside and also noticed my brother's drowsy eyes. I left him to take a rest while I was glued to the window staring at the magnificent and majestic buildings. I saw people moving in a hurry in the dusk as it was after business hours.

Soon we arrived at Kings Cross Station in London for another forty minutes of train ride. Finally, we got off at Colindale Station and walked for further ten minutes to reach my brother's cottage.

As I entered my brother's cottage, I felt the chill. I said to myself, 'Wow, it is cold.'

< 4 > The great expectations of London

Not long after we reached the cottage, Krish suggested I have a shower to freshen up after the journey, and also to warm myself. He showed me where the shower room was and how it worked and warned me to carefully control the temperature of the water. The hot shower was another new experience because I was used to pouring cold water over me with a hand bowl in Malaysia and Singapore, unlike the spray shower in London. That evening's warm shower was a luxury and felt much better than any shower I ever had. As soon as I finished, I changed into my pyjamas and put a jumper on over them.

Following the shower, Krish offered me a cup of hot milk and pointed to my warmed bed before he left the room. Once he was gone, I wondered how to get into the bed, as it had several layers of sheets: bed cover, quilt, blanket, and top and bottom bed sheets. I remembered his earlier instruction on how to tuck myself in to warm up. I followed his advice and found that while the bed was chilly when I first got in, it soon became warmer with my body heat. I had never slept in a proper bed, only on hard surfaces (concrete or wooden floors) on a straw mat. I felt the joy of sleeping on a mattress for the first time. I can remember that night I was so comfortable, warm and relaxed that it did not take me long to forget about my long day and close my eyes.

In the morning Krish woke me up before he left the house to say that I should be able to buy my own lunch as there were many restaurants nearby in Colindale. As I was half asleep when he spoke to me, I nodded my head to signal I had heard. Once he had left, I could not resist my sleepy eyes, and again

I went into a deep slumber. When I opened my eyes again and peeped through the window to check the weather, it looked dull and cloudy, not sunny at all. I was still feeling drowsy, but when I checked the time it was 12.30pm. Very reluctantly I forced myself to get out of that comfortable, warm bed and don a borrowed dressing gown.

The cold bedroom had no sun coming through the window. I still had my woollen top over my pyjamas, but my hands, face and feet were cold. I turned the heating up higher to warm up the place because everything I touched in the room was cold. I forced myself to quickly change into warm clothes as I planned to tackle the outside world.

As I stepped outside the cottage into the cold weather and shut the door, it dawned on me that I had arrived in the UK and I was in London! This was the moment I had waited for most of my life. I thanked my god, Lord Ganesh, for creating this opportunity for me. I told myself that I had to think of the future and make use of the opportunities that had been offered. From that very moment I was prepared to do the hard work necessary to be successful in life.

Outside the house the footpath was icy and I had to be careful with every step I took. I felt the icy breeze on my face and my ears were chilled, but luckily, I had a scarf on and a hat to cover my head. I had borrowed my brother's old gloves and his waterproof overcoat for the weather as advised by him, but I still felt the chilly breeze that blew over my face every few minutes.

I became aware of the very strange, new environment around me. I was no longer in my comfort zone! I was slightly

< 4 > The great expectations of London

anxious and felt a bit strange. The brick houses I walked past looked different to Malaysian houses. They had a small main entrance in the front with a little balcony, and I admired the beautifully manicured gardens with their small courtyards and trimmed hedges. The neat row of trees along the footpath had no leaves because of the approaching winter months.

I observed very different-looking people as I walked. Apart from Europeans, there were several people who had very dark skin and others who appeared to be Chinese. Almost all of the passers-by looked well dressed, but seldom acknowledged each other. When I spoke to the first passer-by, he did not look at me or utter a word in reply. The second passer-by also did not respond to my well wishes. Although there were many people in the wide streets but none of them were talking or looking at anyone, unlike Malaysia or Singapore where acknowledging passers-by was common.

Another striking difference was the street signs. There was so much information and so many directions on street posts: place names, speed limits, upcoming junctions, the distance to the next train, how far to the Tube stations, the names of nearby parks, etcetera. These signs were very useful for newcomers. Luckily, cars drove on the left-hand-side of the road like Malaysia, so I was comfortable as a pedestrian.

My main reason for leaving the cottage that afternoon was to see how London suburbs looked and to buy my lunch. I was not sure where to go, but stopped when I saw a Chinese restaurant across the street. I crossed the road, walked slowly up to the restaurant and started reading the menu displayed in front of the building. As I was reading, one of the waiters approached me and asked if I needed any assistance. I didn't see him approach and was taken aback. Although he was trying to help, I suddenly got nervous and walked away without going in. I wondered why I had behaved so strangely. I think, I was overwhelmed. I was all alone on my first day in a strange, new country. Plus, prior to today, I had not seen that many Europeans dressed so differently from what I was used to, living differently to how I had lived, nor had I thought about what a Chinese restaurant in London would look like. I returned home without my lunch. When my brother came home and asked me how I had enjoyed lunch, I made up an excuse, but did not reveal the true reason for not eating.

After work that evening, my brother was excited about taking me to visit one of his close friends who worked as a part-time chef in a popular London restaurant. His friend was looking forward to my visit as he wanted to surprise me with a very special, large Apple Pie. Several of his friends had also decided to join the Apple Pie party in my honour. They welcomed me and everyone was very excited to see the huge Apple Pie; we could barely wait for it to cool. It was the first time I had seen an Apple Pie, and it was enormous. As the guest of honour, I was given the first slice to eat. Unfortunately, after my first bite, I couldn't eat any more. I was unaccustomed to the taste, so I gave the rest to my brother to finish. I was surprised to see the others finish the entire pie within twenty minutes.

Something similar happened the first time I tasted homemade Spaghetti Bolognaise. One weekend, when my brother, keen to share his culinary talents with me, decided to

< 4 > The great expectations of London

cook a special meal, "spaghetti and mincemeat". He finished work early and came home in a cheery mood with his shopping. He told me about the cuisine and how he had found out about it while studying. It only took him an hour to prepare the dish. He suggested I should have my shower before he served dinner, and when I returned to the dinner table there was a glass of red wine already waiting for me. The plates and cutlery were all set before he served the meal. Again, that was the first time I had seen spaghetti. I thought it was like the long noodles I had eaten in the Chinese restaurants in Malaysia. As he served me, he added more cheese to give it a better taste. As I had not eaten spaghetti, beef or cheese previously, I did not enjoy the food at all but ate a little because I was hungry.

The London underground transport was another new experience for me. In my three months in London, I had carefully observed how to find my way using the London Tube guides. It took me a couple of days to learn my way around London, but as soon as I knew how to use it, my fear and panic about travelling in and around London disappeared. I appreciated and marvelled at the convenience of swift travel in crowded London.

I was aware that my time in London was only short because my destination was Dundee, which was further north in Scotland. In my three months in London I managed to visit several places of interest including Hyde Park, London Tower, Buckingham Palace, Trafalgar Square and many more.

My brother's semester break was coming to an end; he had to return to Dundee University to continue his degree and I had to commence my nursing around the same time.

Although I was relieved that I was following him as he knew the culture and the places of Scotland very well, I was still not quite relaxed.

‹ 5 ›

Embracing Scottish culture

I was very excited and looking forward to my journey to Dundee. I could not believe that I would soon be on my way.

The night before the journey, I was so excited I couldn't sleep. The next morning, as we walked into the London railway station, I noticed how enormous it was. There were several trains leaving, while others were pulling into the station. It was very busy and very noisy. All the train information was clearly displayed on boards for the public, and there were also regular announcements over the loudspeakers about arrivals and departures. These were all in English, but I could not understand what they were saying as the London accent was too strange to my ears, so my brother explained them to me. When we found our train and boarded, my brother said that we were lucky to get seats in the reserved compartment because we had not made any reservations.

I found the compartments clean and warm and the seats very comfortable. The people in my compartment were friendly and started talking as the journey progressed. They were interested to know why we were going to Dundee. I was glad my brother was with me as I could not understand any of their questions because of their accents.

As the sun was rising, the beautiful countryside became clearer and we could see the farm animals grazing, some of them even watching us as the train passed. I noticed the farms had clear boundaries with piled stones cemented together as walls. The natural boundaries also had well-marked hedges to prevent the animals from trespassing and escaping. Overall, the railway journey to Dundee was pleasant.

From the station we took a cab to the apartment with all our luggages. The journey was only twenty minutes, but it spared us carrying our heavy suitcases in the cold weather on icy streets. The streets were busy as it was around November and many of the locals had started their Christmas shopping. There were several stores with sale signs on the windows. We saw several Santa Claus figures around the city as we passed through. The taxi continued its journey from tar-surfaced roads to cobbled roads; the first time I had seen a cobbled street in my life. The buildings quickly changed one kilometre out of the city; they looked older but still seemed solid, just in need of some refurbishment. The streets were much quieter with fewer vehicles on the road. Finally, the taxi came to a halt at an unattractive, old, run-down building at the corner of the street. It looked as if it ought to have been pulled down!

I was not worried by the state of the building, but it was my first experience in a Scottish dwelling. My brother collected his things and I quickly followed him carrying mine until I

< 5 > Embracing Scottish culture

lost sight of him on the circular staircase with poor lighting. It was a two-bedroom apartment on the third floor of a run-down building in Peddi Street, Dundee. As I entered the apartment, it was icy cold and I noticed only one gas heater and an outside toilet. The carpets were worn out and windows were shuddering against the howling wind outside the building. The bedrooms had very basic linen covers on the wood-framed beds. The kitchen had a geyser for hot water, but there were no bathrooms or laundry areas in the apartment. I suspected that the apartment was all my brother could afford, so I accepted it gracefully.

He explained later that he had been living in the university's halls of residence, but they were expensive. My brother knew that I could not stay in the university accommodation as a guest with him, so he had secured this apartment prior to my arrival. I was glad to have his guardianship and support, but was concerned about how my life had swung back under his control again. My fear had returned and I was nervous about when he would resume his outbursts. As the older brother with total domination over me, I knew I couldn't explain to him how I was feeling as he wasn't interested. From the moment we arrived in that apartment, he began directing me as to what I had to do. I even had to wait until he told me I should go to sleep. I often got out of bed as soon as I heard him shout. While I was still familiaring myself with Scottish culture, I tried my best not to make any mistakes, but also lived in a constant state of anxiety.

Comprehending the local terminology was an early challenge for me. I remember that one day my brother was in the toilet and yelled out to me to go to the street corner shop on the ground level to get the rolls. That cold morning at 7.00am, I had to quickly jump out of my bed to run downstairs to the shop. I repeated as exactly as I could what I had heard he had said to the shop-owner', 'Please may I have some rolls?'

Although there was a long queue of customers waiting to be served, the cashier quickly attended to me. I was very pleased with the prompt service and returned to the apartment within minutes, feeling good about my swiftness. I quickly handed the bag to my brother, but within seconds I heard him yelling and swearing at me, shouting, 'You are a stupid idiot. You do not even know how to buy toilet rolls'.

I soon understood the mistake I made as I had bought morning rolls instead of "toilet rolls". I had to quickly run down to the shop to fix the problem.

Another very uncomfortable moment for me was when he sent me to buy lamb meat as he wanted to cook curry. I managed to find a butcher before they closed and returned home with the lamb. When he opened the packet prior to putting the meat into the pot, he turned wild with anger. He demanded to know what I had asked the butcher for. I repeated the same words that I thought I heard, 'Could I have a kilogram of sliced lamb'. He then realised that I did not know the difference between "sliced" and "diced" meat. I quickly ran to the toilet and wept there for a while to calm down.

I can vividly remember my first day at the Ninewells College of Nursing and Midwifery. The apartment was not close to my nursing college and I had to walk for five minutes to catch the bus and then walk for another ten minutes to reach

< 5 > Embracing Scottish culture

the college. In total it took about forty-five minutes. I arrived late as I did not know how long it would take to get there by bus. As I arrived, I was directed by the staff on where to hang my overcoat before I entered the class. As I entered, I noticed that there were mainly Europeans and only four Chinese-looking students. I quickly scanned my eyes for a vacant seat. All the seats were taken except one, but it was next to a girl! I stood at the door for a few moments and looked again to see if there was any other spot available that was not next to a girl. My hesitation came from my very reserved upbringing where I had not been allowed to mix with girls. I guessed that as a late arrival I had to take the only available seat. I had not sat next to a girl since primary school, so I felt incredibly nervous, but I had to put on a brave face. I also had to overcome my cultural shock on seeing so many strange faces in such a small space. I did not turn my head to see any others in the class, but kept my head straight and eyes focused on the instructor who was presenting the lesson at the front of the class.

About an hour later, when I had calmed down a little, I slowly looked around in the class and noticed that the majority of students were girls. In the 1970s, nursing was a popular profession for women, but not men. There were only six males in a class of fifty-four students. Apart from three older-looking students, the rest of them were younger than me.

In my early days, I had to make several personal adjustments to survive in the Scottish culture. I realised in the first three months that my verbal communication was not great. Firstly, I found the strong Scottish accent difficult to comprehend even though I tried my best. After the first few days of frustration, I was courageous enough to ask my Scottish classmates to repeat their sentences slowly so that I could follow their conversation. They had no problem understanding what I said, but I had difficulty understanding them. Many times, my classmates often politely corrected me on how I should pronounce words. I was very grateful to one particular classmate, Ken Shaw, who assisted me often. His continued help definitely improved my pronunciation and reduced my stress while adjusting to the new environment. We became very good buddies and spent a lot of time together. His six-foot tall, well-built body definitely protected me and he often intervened when he noticed anyone attempting to bully me. He wanted to make sure that I was treated with respect and not harmed because of my cultural differences. There were occasions when he raised his voice to drinkers in pubs to warn them to be respectful towards me. In one incident, Ken pointed his finger at the perpetrator and said, 'He is my brother from Dundee and I am his protector. If anyone here disturbs him, be careful.' When I heard this, I felt I truly had a guardian in Scotland and was one hundred percent at ease whenever I was in a pub with him.

I had to learn the expected Scottish table etiquette, which was different to Malaysia. As a cosmopolitan nation, Malaysian Malays, Chinese and Indians, rice is their staple food. The Indians usually served the rice on a plate with all accompaniments before they started eating with their fingers. They were used to eating hot and spicy food with lots of gravy and they often had tap water handy. The Malays also ate very hot and spicy food with their fingers, but not often with gravy.

The Chinese would scoop their food from the bowl into their mouth with chopsticks. The Chinese dishes were usually fried, not hot or spicy, and usually eaten as soon as they were cooked.

Fingers and chopsticks were not in common usage in Scotland; instead they used forks and knives. When I went for lunch in the dining hall at the nursing school between lectures, I had to pick up the appropriate cutlery before being seated. Even choosing the right spoon for dessert or soup was confusing at the beginning. Although I had used a knife and fork on the plane, I still needed practice to eat confidently in public.

One of the expected eating habits in Scotland was chewing food with your mouth closed, unlike Malaysian culture. Many Malaysians chewed their food with their mouths open and slurped while drinking. It was also common to talk during meals as it was the only chance families had to catch up with one another. Malaysian meal times were not quiet moments!

When I was in Scotland, I was comfortable eating all meat dishes except beef, which took me a while to introduce into my diet. I was brought up as a conservative Hindu, so eating beef was a cultural taboo. My mother had warned me not to eat beef at any cost because cows were considered sacred. Nearly all practising Hindus in the world refrain from eating beef, even if they eat chicken and lamb. All seafood was acceptable to eat, but pork was forbidden, although not as strongly as beef.

When I was in Scotland, I realised beef was on most menus. To start with, I avoided it, choosing from the dishes that didn't include it (which were often vegetarian). After a few months had passed, I intentionally began to include beef in my diet. The first few times I ate it, it tasted strange to me, and my mum's warning flashed in my mind. After these meals, I prayed hard and asked for forgiveness as I was doing something against my religion, and more importantly, disobeying my mum's wish.

One of the chores I did not mind doing was grocery shopping, because most of the items were wrapped on the shelves and ready to be picked up without spending too much time selecting. Also, customers in Scotland wait in the queue to be served unlike Malaysia.

The supermarket staff were always courteous and respectful. The staff at the service desk often came to talk to shoppers and assist them if they saw anyone looking for something for a while or needed help. Such customer focus made my shopping feel easy in Scotland.

Public transport was also very different. In Scotland, passengers often waited for the bus in a queue and the frail, sick, elderly or pregnant travellers were given seat priority, whereas taking public transport in Malaysia was stressful. Every time I had taken the bus, it was uncomfortable because of the pushing that occurred to secure a seat, with little attention paid to frail or old people.

In the winter months, I had to use the public restrooms quite often, but I never hesitated to do so because they were well maintained by the local government. Their toilets were regularly checked to ensure they were in working order and there was no strong ammonia odour. Unfortunately, there was no tap next to the seat for water to wash oneself, only paper for wiping. I had to adjust from the wet way to the "new" dry way.

Initially, I felt very unclean without water to wash my bottom, but I slowly became accustomed to the quick way.

While living in Dundee and adjusting to the Scottish culture, my brother decided we should move out to our own residences. I felt that God had been listening to me when both our applications were successful and I was counting my days for the move.

The moment I moved to live at Ninewells, I began to relax. The residence rooms were located in the same building as the college. Classes were conducted on the top floor while the ground level had the residence and dining halls, as well as sports and recreational facilities. The new, fully-furnished facility was centrally heated, unlike the cold Dundee apartment. The facility included a hot shower, kitchen, a comfortable lounge with chairs and tables, an indoor toilet and a laundry room to be shared by four residents in each unit. The rooms had built-in wardrobes with shelving and a long study table with a lamp. The single bed had a firm and comfortable mattress. The bed linen was changed daily and the building was cleaned by contracted cleaners.

The sports and entertainment facilities at the residence were very well-equipped. There were T.V. rooms, games facilities (for table tennis, board/card games, squash courts) and a swimming pool with shower facilities. I felt the college residence was a luxury for me compared to the dilapidated Peddi Street apartment. The subsidised rent was affordable and was deducted from my monthly allowance.

I used everything the residence offered. Most evenings I exercised before my meals, swimming or playing squash. In the evenings, after my meals, I went to the common rooms to relax, watch T.V. or to socialise with my fellow residents.

One small limiting factor with the college residence was the strict rules. The warden in the residence worked from 7.00am until 6.00pm, with continuous surveillance to ensure the rules were followed. When the warden left at 6.00pm, the front door of the residence was locked until they returned at 7.00am. For safety reasons, all residents had to sign out when they left, and they had to note their expected time of return. Furthermore, no males were allowed to enter the female apartments. All lights and loud music had to be turned off by midnight.

Despite those rules, living in the residence was a great fun time for me. I appreciated its comforts because I had not had such luxurious accommodation when I was growing up.

Most of the local students in the residence went home on weekends, so the place was quiet. They often left on Friday evenings and returned on Monday mornings, so sometimes I felt very lonely, but I was also glad to have free time to myself.

One day my Malaysian friend, Gana, mentioned that he had been asked by a group of nursing students to come over for a meal at their hospital residence. These four girls regularly cooked traditional Malaysian food and I was happy to be invited so soon after settling in.

In Scotland in the 1970s, it was not easy to find restaurants that served traditional Asian meals, so I was pleased when I heard about the invitation. Gana was not keen to go to dinner at first, but I convinced him to come along, as I had been dreaming about Malaysian food from the moment we were invited. We made a deal: if Gana did not enjoy their company,

< 5 > Embracing Scottish culture

we would return at once to Ninewells. However, as the evening proceeded, I saw Gana was enjoying their company and we did not rush back to Ninewells.

A week later we met the four girls again. The two Indians were called Mano and Suba, and the other two girls, Ming and Angie, were Chinese. The four girls resided in one of the nurse's quarters at Maryfield Hospital, which was about fifteen kilometres from Ninewells College. When Gana and I were seconded to do our twelve-week clinical training at Maryfield Hospital, we often dropped in and waited in the visitor's room for cooked meals after work.

We never brought any food to share with the girls. Retrospectively, I realised we could have done some shopping before we went over, but Malaysian custom stated it was rude to bring food when you are invited over for a meal. The only way to show our appreciation for their dinners was to invite them in return for a meal at our residence, which we did much later.

There was no doubt that the girls were far better cooks than us. They often took time preparing the main menu for the evening, organising the correct combination of different dishes, while what we cooked was easy and quick. The girls usually cooked Chinese cuisine with rice and plenty of vegetables, whereas we did mainly rice with meat curry. Gana had not cooked in his life, so most of the cooking was done by me, while he often ended up washing the dishes after the meals instead. All six of us would talk about very general things, such as places in Malaysia, our school experiences, our favourite foods, etcetera.

Gana was slim-built, agile and a keen sportsman. He had previously played hockey for his school in Malaysia and played badminton at the local club in Dundee. He often encouraged us all to go to the games room for either a game of table tennis or cards, followed by board games, before we finished the night with a hot drink.

We had a lot of fun with the girls and we enjoyed their company. As our friendship grew closer, we went on group excursions. During summer we went to the movies, the beach, nearby castles and on horse riding trips. Gana and I looked forward to their invitations so that we could catch up with them. Our earlier visits to the residence were mainly to enjoy their cooking, while their company was a secondary benefit. Slowly that feeling changed.

Amongst the four girls, I was interested in one of them: Suba (Subatra). Although Suba was a Malaysian Indian like me, we did not speak the same dialect. She spoke Malayalam, the native language of the people from the Indian State of Kerala, whereas I spoke Tamil. She had learned Tamil through her Tamil-speaking housemaid while growing up. It was very uncomfortable to talk or discuss any personal matters with the four girls. Sharing my terrible personal history was very uncomfortable for me with my very reserved upbringing. Although I was in my twenties, my social skills were extremely limited. I was not comfortable asking any girl on a date, not even Suba. I was so reserved that I did not know what couples did when they were on a date. I had heard many of my friends mention dating, but I did not quite comprehend what they were for or how to arrange one.

< 5 > Embracing Scottish culture

During the holidays I seized the opportunity to use my free time to work towards my ambitions, as most of the nursing students had gone home and the residence was quiet. During those times, I was up around 6.00am and did my regular morning exercises, such as swimming or running, and had a shower before breakfast. By 10.00am, I began my private study on advanced biology, chemistry and physics, as those subjects were the pre-requisite for university admission. I often used the large games room as my study when there was no one to distract me.

One evening, I thought there was no one else around, but I saw Suba walk past me in her blue jeans to the residence T.V. room. Observing her carefully for the first time, I noticed she had beautiful, long hair. Although we had talked many times in the company of other Malaysians, we did not take any personal interest in each other; we simply enjoyed the group meals. She must have realised that I was "stuck" in the residence on college lecture breaks, just like her because she suddenly dropped into the games room where I was studying. We spoke about our family backgrounds, but not about ourselves. After an interesting conversation, she left me without any arrangements to meet again. I was keen to see her again but was too shy to ask her for a date.

On my second encounter, I asked Suba to go for a walk, saying that I needed a break from my studies. As arranged, we went for our first walk in the cold, dark winter. At that time, the Scottish winter had begun, but I had not prepared for the season because I had no intention of going out in the cold. Although I had a pair of comfortable boots for walking, they were not suitable for icy conditions. I had minimal winter clothes to wrap around myself. I only had a pair of jeans and a pullover with an anorak to keep me warm, unlike the locals who were warmly dressed in winter jackets, leather boots and scarves to keep the cold out. The dark, winter evening was helpful because we were not comfortable being seen together in public. On occasions we walked for two to three hours in the quiet, cold nights admiring our surroundings under the moonlight and finding excuses to hug each other to keep ourselves warm.

As time passed, all four girls, (Mano, Angie, Ming and Suba), Gana and I found excuses to meet regularly to celebrate our birthdays or any other events that we could think of. Suba and I kept our meetings very private and did not disclose them to anyone, not even to the group of four. When Suba and I met privately after college hours, we ensured that we were out of sight of anyone from the residence or hospital. During our initial meetings we just sat and talked about ourselves. Suba was very keen to know what my intentions were for the future. I was honest and explained that I wanted to do my degree but had no financial support for my education. As for Suba, who, unlike me, came from a poverty-free background, had the opportunity to embark on any further studies she wished. As we continued enjoying each other's company, we shared more about our differences and ambitions. We both looked forward to our walks and began holding hands and hugging each other, only partly due to the cold weather!

The time between our dates was harder and harder to endure. Soon, I began to question myself, *Why am I becoming*

5 Embracing Scottish culture

very fond of this girl? What would my family say if I told them that I had found a girlfriend? I knew my mother would be shocked and would not welcome the idea of me having a girlfriend, nor to know that she was from a different caste than her.

I slowly began to understand that Suba's background was very different to mine. Suba was the only girl in her family and was brought up as her father's favourite. She spoke with confidence and was quite vocal on issues that she strongly believed in. Meanwhile, I was the youngest in the family and had fended for myself from a very young age. I did not have much confidence like Suba. As the only girl, her family did not suppress her from expressing her views openly, while I lacked the confidence to put my point of view forward because my family did not consider my views important. Furthermore, I was the youngest in my family and most of the time I had been told what I should do, with no explanation; I was just ordered to follow their advice. My family did not give me the opportunity to develop my self-esteem, and what little self-esteem I held was diminished by my oldest brother. Suba soon realised the background differences between us.

As Suba and I got to know each other more, she began to understand my circumstances and the reasons that had led me to nursing. She understood that nursing would begin my career path and I had aspirations, even though at the time the profession of "male nurse" was not valued in Indian culture. Traditionally, Indians are very status-conscious, and my family was no exception. They preferred occupations such as a doctor, lawyer, engineer, or barrister for men; not being a nurse.

When my girlfriend and I were getting to know each other more closely, my brother started contacting me. Suba came to know more about him from me. His regular calls were usually asking for financial help, as his savings from holiday work had run out before his semester had finished. He was aware that I received a small monthly allowance while nursing. This allowance was hardly enough for me, but I was obliged to help him because of his help during my younger days. On certain occasions, he expected more than I could afford and, as a result, I had to struggle for survival.

He demanded that I come over to his residence during my nursing lecture breaks, which stressed me. I was very uncomfortable resting at his place on my off days. I felt that the lecture-free days that I had been looking forward to had come to an abrupt halt because of his demands. He still wanted to maintain his authoritative control over me. He must have believed that older members of the family, like him, had every right to impose their power over the younger members of the family. On the days when I reluctantly stayed at his place, he still yelled and shouted at me for any small mistakes. I felt hurt, and once again his behaviour made me very uncomfortable and nervous. I felt completely dominated. He made sure he reinforced the fear he had instilled in me when I was living with him in Malaysia. I found his behaviour quite astounding and was surprised his character had not changed despite him living in the UK for six years. I had expected him to be reasonable and treat me with some respect as I had grown older, but I was disappointed instead.

‹ 6 ›
Surviving Dundee's challenges

While I was working as nurse, I still had the burning desire to further my education through university. I realised that I would take three years to complete my nursing and another four years to complete a degree. I also needed another year to study the university entrance course before I could commence my university education. Entry into Scottish University required Advanced Level (A level) or Scottish Higher Grades.

Achieving the required university entry grades was not going to be easy for me because I had not studied after my secondary education in Malaysia. Most of the students who did the university entrance studies would have progressed from primary to secondary school on a continuous study path without any interruption to their education. My study gaps happened because of my challenging circumstances, but it meant I would be about ten years older than most students doing the university entrance course.

Studying was difficult, especially when English was not

my first language. I had not read many books because I could not afford to buy books for leisure. In my primary school days, I did not really socialise with children my age, or have a mentor or guardian at home to help with my reading. I had to hand-wash my own clothes, cook my own meals and collect firewood, etcetera. Although I had not had time to read books, luckily I still managed to complete my primary school education.

Apart from the age difference, I also had a knowledge gap in my basic sciences. In my secondary education in Malaysia I had studied General Certificate of Education at Ordinary (O) levels; including English, General Mathematics and General Science, but no pure sciences such as Physics, Chemistry, Biology or Mathematics. My plan to do pure sciences at university entrance level without secondary school science knowledge was a bit ambitious.

I found out that only Kingsway Technical College (KTC) in Dundee offered science courses to prepare students for tertiary studies, but they only ran during the day, and KTC was not near my Ninewells residence. I had to catch two buses and then walk to attend, but I was determined to attempt my A Levels and Scottish Higher Grades. Despite these obstacles, I contacted KTC to ask about enrolling.

Following my enquiry, I was referred to speak to the department head. The Head of Mathematics and Sciences Department, Mr David Hamilton, understood my desire to study and endorsed my application to commence my studies without hesitation. He knew my prior learning background as a pure Arts student was insufficient to bridge my science knowledge gap and that this course would help. He was supportive, but warned me that attempting to do science at university entrance level would be an uphill battle. I took his advice seriously and promised him that I would do my best.

Mr Hamilton advised me that it would be impossible for me to complete the course successfully unless I studied it full time. This was impossible for me as I had not completed my nursing and was in no position to support myself for full-time study on student nurse wages. Mr Hamilton, who knew my circumstances, was willing to help me with my application for a City of Dundee study sponsorship. With his recommendation, the City awarded me a twelve-month full-time study grant with free tuition at the KTC.

I was quite excited to commence my studies, but the new classes and my nursing course overlapped by two months. The university entrance classes (A Level and Scottish Higher Grades) commenced in August, but my nursing classes did not finish until early October. The education grant was awarded upon the condition that I was enrolled in full-time study and attended all classes from Monday to Friday, while my UK visa was for my nursing studies, which I had to complete otherwise I had to leave the country. Therefore, I had to start my full-time A Level studies while completing my nursing. I, somehow, had to manage the two months of full-time study in both courses, as I could not afford to let go of either of them.

Doing the two courses at the same time was a very challenging period in my life. Every day I had to follow my planned schedule so that I did not miss either course. My strategy to attend the A Level study was to use my flexible nursing shift hours and the two off days every week from nursing. Luckily, those two months of the nursing course were on hospital practicum, without theory sessions to attend.

I requested the hospital to roster my shifts on weekday afternoons, so I was able to attend the A Level classes in the mornings. I attended classes from 9.00am to midday Monday to Friday and worked afternoon shifts at the hospitals. Most weekends I was in the clinical areas I had requested, and with these arrangements I covered my nursing shifts and the required attendance at KTC.

It was a race against time for the two months. I had to leave home at 8.00am, allowing one hour for bus travel to my 9.00am class at KTC. I often left my class around 11.45am for my afternoon shift, which finished around 9.30pm. By then, I was totally exhausted. I was grateful to my teachers who understood my situation and permitted me to leave my class early to get to hospital for my practicum.

On the few occasions I missed the bus, I had to run to the clinical areas to be on time. On those "rushed" days, I had to miss my lunch. Sometimes, I missed the nursing handover from the nursing head when staff changeover took place, but luckily one of the nurses updated me privately on the missed patient information.

Finally, the two months of juggling with my full-time studies in two courses came to an end. I completed my three-year nursing course successfully, while my A Level studies continued until I completed my examinations.

I felt great achieving my very first professional qualification in nursing. I hoped it created an opportunity to earn an income to assist my future studies. I was also very relieved when I finished my nursing course, because from then on, I was able to concentrate on my university entrance studies. Continuing studies at KTC without rushing to the hospital for my nursing shifts was a great relief.

Finishing my nursing course was a relief, but I had to give up the comfortable Ninewells residence I had enjoyed during my studies. The only affordable accommodation available at the time was at the City Council of Dundee Commission apartments in Whitfield, a suburb of Dundee.

I shifted my few belongings to the one-bedroom Housing Commission apartment in Whitfield, about 20km from the city. It was not convenient for college, but I had no choice. Following the Council's assessment, my weekly rent was £5. The one-bedroom apartment was sufficient, with a living room, kitchenette, bathroom and indoor toilet, and it was also close to the public bus stop. It suited my basic needs, as I had no intention of spending a lot of time in the flat.

The unfurnished flat had no curtains or blinds, but had big windows which I kept covered with some old blankets. I had to purchase a few basic essential items for the apartment, including a wooden chair and a table for my study. For the kitchen, I purchased a big aluminium pot, a deep-frying pan, a ladle and some cutlery. The total cost for purchasing my basic second-hand household things had to be under £20. I was lucky to find an old bed with a mattress that was left in the flat. There were also some built-in shelves in the bedroom for my few clothes.

The apartment was primarily for my studies, as I had no time to relax until I finished my A Levels. I refrained from purchasing a television, radio, comfortable sofa, etcetera, because I was afraid entertainment or relaxation would reduce my study time. I knew these strict restrictions I put on myself were only temporary, but I could not afford to ruin the one-time opportunity I had been offered. The sacrifice I made at that point in my life was difficult, but I was determined to gain a place to do my degree.

The local government grant covered the tuition fees for my studies, but I still needed to earn some cash for basic living. Luckily, with my good student nursing record, I managed to get a weekend position as a Registered Nurse (RN) at Ninewells Hospital without any trouble.

When my classes were over on Friday at 5.00pm, I would rush home to cook and finish my dinner as soon as I could, so that I could rest for a while before I left for the night shift that commenced at 9.15pm. I had to report at 8.45pm to the Nursing Officer who would then direct me to a specific ward/unit to work. When the shift ended on Saturday morning at 7.30am, I would be home by 9.30am following patient information handover to the morning shift nurses. I would rush home to my desperately needed sleep till 2pm. Following the sleep, I would complete my A Level homework and revise my college lectures. After an early dinner, I would rest for Saturday night before I started my shift again and when that finished, I would be home by 9.30am. I avoided the Sunday night shifts because my Monday morning lectures commenced at 9.00am. I accepted extra shifts during college

< 6 > Surviving Dundee's challenges

breaks and holidays to earn more cash, but not during the semester.

The weekend shifts were always busy and, in some ways, I considered the work a form of diversion therapy from my academic work. I found myself totally absorbed in caring for my patients. The supportive nursing team at the hospital often brought snacks and food from their homes to share with me, as they knew that I was attending college full-time with limited income. Sometimes I took my college notes to work with the hope of finding time to read them, but usually ended up bringing them back without opening them. The night shift hours often flew past very quickly because I was always busy and seldom sat down when I was on duty. The only moments I had to sit was to write my patient condition reports around 4.30 in the morning.

While on duty, my few minutes of free time were spent reading medical journals to update myself. Sometimes I read medical journals in hospital library before work. Many of my colleagues, particularly the juniors, often looked forward to my clinical tutorials on the latest information from the new medical journals. Slowly, I cultivated enquiring minds amongst staff and students, encouraging them to question the rationale for every clinical action. Several of the personal care nursing assistants, who had not completed any formal health education, were very keen to improve their knowledge in health when I was working with them. During the short breaks on the nights, I often conducted some special sessions for them as a part of our caring team. As a recently qualified active Registered Nurse (RN) at the time with sound basic science knowledge, I was able to quench their thirst for knowledge.

As a late starter in science, I had to work harder than others. In order to fully understand the concepts, I constantly read books on those topics after lectures. I found the A Level practical classes in science difficult because I had to set up the experiments, conduct them and also submit reports on a weekly basis for assessment. My lack of prior knowledge in science was a limiting factor, so the college library became my second home during the week, while my apartment was only there to prepare my meals, eat, sleep and do some study.

My weekly routine was set: attend classes from Monday to Friday, spend time in the library after my lectures, come home late in the evenings, and go to work on Friday and Saturday nights. On Saturday and Sunday afternoons I woke up at 1.00pm and finished my college notes revision by 2.00pm.

One could say I had a boring life during my A Levels because I did not spare any time to socialise; I deliberately spent my time with studies as my highest priority.

I managed my expenses carefully. My meals were very simple to keep costs down: before I went to college each morning, I prepared about eight slices of bread with butter and jam from home. I ate two pieces at the morning tea breaks, four pieces at lunch and another two pieces for an evening snack. At times, I was too hungry and finished them all at lunch and nothing was left for the evening snack. Sometimes, I had no choice but to spend my limited cash to buy food for the evening.

Once a week I cooked a pot full of gravy to eat with rice

and bread and rationed the food to last me at least for the next three days. I had no fridge, but my kitchen was cold enough to leave food without refrigeration. I economised by purchasing local vegetables when they were on sale.

I kept myself warm so that I did not fall sick. Heating water was costly, but I managed to save on my hot water bills by bathing at the college gymnasium. During the week, after I finished my revision at the library following my lectures, I did some quick exercise at the college gymnasium before my shower. To keep the cost down on weekends after my shift, I also showered at the hospital. Furthermore, the off-peak heating system in my apartment was set to automatically only warm the place at night, which helped to keep my electricity bill down. I seldom turned on the heating and managed to keep my monthly electricity bill at around £5.

Public transport to KTC was not accessible from where I lived and the distance made the fares costly, so I walked the seven-kilometre journey from my flat to college each morning, which took me about eighty minutes. Before I left the flat, I always wrapped myself up warmly and soon the heat generated from walking kept me warm. During the summer months it was a great walk, although there were still cold days that often chilled my body even when I had an anorak on top of my woollen jumper. Sometimes, I had two jumpers on top of my long-sleeved shirt to survive the cold breeze. In winter, the snow-covered surroundings were very picturesque, but the roads and streets were hazardous for pedestrians and vehicles. I had learned to walk carefully after several falls from the slippery, hardened snow.

So, the year before I was admitted to my science degree, my life revolved between college studies and weekend hospital work. I was tired with study-work-study seven days a week during the semester. Occasionally I dreamt about my classmates and wondered how they might be enjoying their free time.

Sometimes when I happened to meet my nursing classmates by chance, they quickly updated me on how well they were living and enjoying their lives with good income from full-time work as RNs. According to them, their monthly income was sufficient for comfortable living with an affordable house and car to commute. They sometimes narrated their exciting adventures and travels, which were interesting to listen to, which I felt was missing in my life. I often guessed that they were not keen to hear about my struggling life in a Housing Commission apartment, where low socio-economic status people lived. When I compared their standard of living with mine, there was a big difference; I hardly had even good clothes to wear and could not afford any kind of leisurely activities. The only thing that kept me going was my strong determination to gain a university place to do my degree.

My limited income, sub-standard home and determination to study had led me to live a boring, dull life, so the sudden visit by Suba, one of the four Malaysian girls, at my apartment lightened me up. She was doing her midwifery at Aberdeen Royal Infirmary about 70km from Dundee.

Sometimes on those weekends, I took sick leave from work to spend my time with her. I fetched her from Dundee

‹ 6 › Surviving Dundee's challenges

Railway station on the local bus. When I knew she was coming, I found it difficult to be waiting for her patiently. Suba and I talked about many issues and more seriously about our future together. When she was with me, we went for walks and listened to the tapes she brought with her, as she knew I had no music in my apartment. We discussed our differences and how our poor communication in the past had created some tension between us and had caused a short-term separation. The ten months of separation made us realise that we had missed each other terribly.

Suba's visits definitely energised me and helped diminish my loneliness. We were both very emotional when she had to return to Aberdeen after spending a couple of days together. Even before I could send her away, my heart became very heavy and I found it hard to talk. When I returned to my apartment after seeing her off, I often cried. I found it hard to concentrate on my studies for the next few hours. To manage my loneliness, I would stay at Gana's place, heading to college from there the next day.

During those stressful days, Gana was not only my close friend but also my saviour. When we finished our nursing studies, I started my university entrance studies at KTC, while he continued to work in nursing. He was very passionate about mental health, so he took on an RN position in psychiatry. He also moved out of the nursing college residence and shared a house with another co-worker. Gana often encouraged me to stay at his place as he didn't live too far from me. When I visited him during those stressful days, I was very relaxed and enjoyed the comforts of his fully furnished house.

Proper furniture to sit on and the allocated spare room with a comfortable bed to sleep on made me appreciate those moments I visited him. His fully equipped kitchen, with all the necessary cutlery and cooking utensils, sometimes lured me to cook Asian meals for him and me.

His washing machine was handy as I often brought all my dirty clothes to wash and iron at his place while I was chatting and sipping his scotch. Reaching Gana's place was not an issue because the bus stopped almost next to his doorstep. When my flat was cold and icy, his place was comfortably warm with central heating. His housemate also worked in mental health and was equally friendly and welcoming. On those days when I felt very lonely or emotionally upset, the time spent at Gana's place saved me not only from boredom, but also recharged my mental wellness.

While I was living at the Housing Commission apartment in Whitfield, I had an unpleasant experience. I was grateful for the support given by the Dundee Council during my financially challenging times, but I was sad to note that many of the residents did not take pride in the apartments provided to them so cheaply. Whitfield was not a well-to-do community as many of them were unemployed and were dependant on social security. I found that the community playgrounds in the suburb were littered with food wrappers, unfinished food, used toys, etcetera. In some parts of the compound there were strong stenches of animal and human excrement. When I walked through the lawn between the apartments, I noticed many resident pet owners did not take care of their animals. Many of their dogs roamed freely in the suburb without a leash, and I was chased by them more than once. They were not trained, and it was not unusual seeing their excrement scattered all over the playground and even on the stairways into the apartments. When I walked through the smelly parts of the suburb, I had to be very careful where I placed my feet.

Although the public bus services to the city and hospitals from Whitfield were excellent, many of the residents in the suburb had their own transport. The local convenience stores had become a meeting place for young cyclists and the only local pub had good business from under-aged drinkers, who were not age-checked as they entered the premises. On occasion, there were noisy domestic scenes in the nearby apartments following alcohol-related family violence episodes.

After I had lived in Whitfield for two months, I decided to get a small scooter to save time travelling from Whitfield to college and work. It only took me twenty minutes to get to my college from my apartment instead of eighty minutes by foot. The vehicle not only saved my travel time, but also increased my resting time. On Fridays I was able to come home early to rest before my night shift at the hospital. Although I had the bike, I preferred to take the bus to work because in the early mornings following the night shifts, I was too tired to ride home. Even in the bus I often fell asleep by the time I got home, so riding home after night shifts was not safe.

The enjoyment of the bike did not last long. One day I found the bike's right mirror was missing and a week later the left mirror was gone. I was very upset with that, so I moved the bike from its usual place to the roadside where I could see it from the kitchen window. As the weather became colder and wetter, I was concerned about the bike rusting. I rented a lock-up garage without making any formal complaints to the Housing Commission about the damage to my bike.

A week later I had a narrow escape from an accident. Someone from the neighbourhood must have spilled oil on the spot of the road where I usually turned the corner. One day, as I took the corner on my bike, I lost control as the wheels slid and hit the curb of the road. I was thrown in the air but was still hanging on to the bike handles. Luckily, I did not suffer much damage because I landed on the grassy pavement.

Following the bike incident, the abuse towards me intensified. The following week there was human excrement on the stairway to the building. The next day I noticed the human excrement in a trail all the way up and next to my apartment door. A week later there was human excrement painted on my apartment wall and door. I was very upset and felt sorry for the people who did that. I was not sure whether they were hoping that I would move out of the apartment, but after those encounters I was more determined not to be perturbed by those incidents but to continue my studies. Sometimes I wondered whether those incidents would have happened if, I had taken the time to know them and socialise with the community.

I was relieved when I completed my A Level examinations and got a full-time position at the Ninewells Hospital rather than the weekend part-time work. I was allowed to choose my favourite unit to work in the day after the interview. I chose to work in the medical wards because I had the most experience in that area.

Although I had worked in the hospital on nights, it still took me a few days to familiarise myself with the ward routines, as the daytime activities were quite different. During the day there were several multidisciplinary teams in the wards and each of them had their own routines that related to the assessment, diagnosis and treatment of clients. Therefore, my responsibilities as an RN were much greater on day shifts than the nights, because I had to support various senior health professionals.

‹ 7 ›

The freedom to make my own decisions

Throughout all of this, I had been applying to universities, and one day I received an offer from Aberdeen University, my first university preference. As soon as I received the offer, I declined the other universities' offers and immediately accepted the one from Aberdeen. I knew the university semester commenced in September and I had to be financially prepared for the study costs, tuition fees and accommodation expenses. I also needed to consider how serious my relationship with Suba was.

While I was working at Ninewells, Suba would come down to Dundee from Aberdeen on Fridays and stayed the weekends with me, returning on Monday mornings. It was during one of those visits that we seriously discussed our future together.

We assessed our situation so that we understood our cultural, financial and career goals and differences. As both of us had been brought up in our own strict sub-cultural ways, we found it difficult to compromise our values. I spoke

< 7 > The freedom to make my own decisions

Tamil and she spoke Malayalam and we were not certain what language would be best to communicate in when we were married and living as husband and wife. Our strong sub-cultural differences might be acceptable to our communities if we were friends, but would not extend to a marriage.

Apart from these differences, our families had greatly influenced us in our thinking and had set our biases. Her family had a marked influence on her: she had three brothers, one older and two younger, whereas I was the baby in my family with two older sisters and three older brothers. Suba, as the only girl in her family, was pampered and allowed to have a say in decisions, whereas I had always been directed about what I had to do. After we came to know each other more closely, we still questioned how we would manage or close the gap that existed between us once we were married.

As we continued our discussion, we began to understand each other better. Suba and I were aware of Hindu arranged marriages that were common at the time in Malaysia. The girl's parents would normally look for men with good education and a permanent job with a good income. Suba, being a beautiful, light-skinned girl, well-spoken with complete self-confidence, had already received proposals from eligible professionals with good incomes, such as doctors, engineers, lawyers and accountants. She had not disclosed to her family that I had appeared in her life, and as she was interested in me, she did not go ahead with those proposals.

I was also still receiving regular calls from my brother Krish, who by then had completed his Engineering degree at Dundee University and was working in London as a full-time

Civil Engineer. He still insisted that I call him every week to explain my "moves". I found it quite insulting to have to explain what I was doing at the age of twenty-seven. I gave him respect as an older brother and telephoned him as he demanded. At the time, I only had access to a coin-operated public telephone down the road from my apartment. To remain outside in the cold winters after my evening shift work was a challenge. Those days it was very dark near the poorly lit telephone booth and it was also unsafe to be out alone after 10.00pm. Furthermore, when we spoke, he would listen to what I had been doing and he always criticised me before we ended our conversation. I usually returned to my apartment very upset and, on occasion, very frustrated after speaking to him. He refused to understand my challenging circumstances at that time. From my childhood till the age of twenty-seven, he had been dominating me and the only reason he left me to do my studies in Dundee was because I received the Dundee City grant. Otherwise, I would have had to follow him to London with his family during my university entrance studies.

His demanding calls to my work started bothering me because he interrupted my concentration in caring for my patients. He was such a domineering character in my life; he expected me to follow what he thought was right for me without realising that I was also an individual and had the right to make my own decisions. I'm sure he was interested in my welfare and wellbeing and as such I had obeyed his command for years with the same fear and anxiety from my childhood.

< 7 > The freedom to make my own decisions

After each call, I had to debrief myself before I returned to work. I was thinking of how to remove his grip on me. One way I thought of was not to communicate with him at all. It may not have been the best option, but I had no one to talk to about the sufferings I had endured all those years.

The hospital policy did not condone any private phone calls by staff, unless it was an emergency. One night I politely advised him to refrain from calling me at work. As I had predicted, he found it very difficult to accept this. He began to raise his voice and spoke to me in a very harsh manner, 'You are a big man now, so you are telling me not to call?'

I reminded him again that I was busy with my patients and had to go. I had to hang up after a few minutes of our phone chat. The following two nights when he tried to reach me, I did not answer his calls. I told my work colleagues that if anyone called for me, they should inform the caller that I was not available. He tried a week later, but I avoided him. A few weeks after he had stopped calling me, I was worried that he was planning to come up to Dundee to threaten me in person. My apprehension subsided as days went by and I did not hear from him. After six weeks, I felt that I had managed to get myself out of his grip. From then on, I began to plan my future according to my way without worrying about his consent. This was the beginning of me making my own decisions!

Suba was aware that getting my undergraduate degree was a prerequisite for the wedding plans. When I received a notice in writing that I had been offered a place at Aberdeen University, we were glad to be able to seriously begin our discussion about our wedding. Sometimes I wondered what would have happened if I not been able to get a place. Would we have continued our relationship and plans?

When she stayed the weekends in Dundee in my dingy accommodation, our marriage was the key conversation topic and we often talked about it non-stop. Our time together was two days with no time spent apart. As we were young and had dreams to live together, we reaffirmed that we had become fond of each other and had decided to settle down. We had both expressed how we missed each other while I was doing my university entrance studies in Dundee and Suba was working as a midwife in Aberdeen.

We talked about our differences and attempted to compromise, but we were concerned about how to announce to our families our intention to marry. Suba's news would surprise her family because she had always avoided the topic whenever it was brought up.

Secondly, her family would not be happy about her prospective groom's-to-be with poor credentials. I had just finished my nursing qualification and did not have a degree. Suba was aware that according to her family, nursing was the last choice as a career. I was also financially poor and had no rich relatives to boost my status. Suba was worried about how her family would react to her unsuitable groom. Suba had received proposals from various eligible professionals that her mother and her younger brother, Raji, were interested in, but Suba had turned them down.

Suba had to give them the news and hope that they would accept her decision. Her older brother (Faisal) and sister-in-law knew us from five years back when Suba and I

< 7 > The freedom to make my own decisions

were courting in Dundee. Faisal was an undergraduate civil engineering student at Glasgow University, at that time, and we had visited them on our days off. Both his wife and he knew our situation and had always welcomed us. Suba's sister-in-law was a Muslim, totally outside the Hindu culture. Faisal, as a non-Muslim, had to face strict Islamic rituals prior to his wedding. We hoped that their endorsement would help avoid objections to our marriage. Despite their support, Suba and I were very anxious of how the extended families would react upon hearing of her Tamil groom.

Although Suba and I had planned our wedding, I decided not to inform my family members right away. I knew that my relatives would be disappointed finding out that I had planned the wedding without including them in the discussions. As I was the youngest of six children, my siblings would have liked to have been involved. Normally, Hindu wedding arrangements take a minimum of one year to plan after the official engagement ceremony. Suba and I decided on a six-month plan.

As we did not have families involved, it was easier for us to eliminate some of the longer traditional protocols about the expected attributes of the bride and groom and how well they matched according to Hindu astrology. We also bypassed the serious discussion about wedding dress items, jewellery for the bride and the sharing of wedding expenses between the groom's and bride's families.

For our engagement, I only purchased a diamond ring before Suba went to Malaysia. I also saved a small amount of cash from my short-term work in order to purchase the wedding sari and ring in Malaysia. I did not purchase anything for myself, not even a traditional basic Indian costume for the wedding. At the same time, I did not promise to buy anything for anyone for the wedding and would clearly brief my family and future in-laws not to expect anything from me. Suba left for Malaysia, and we decided that I would follow in six months.

According to our plans, I had only three weeks in Malaysia before I had to return to UK to commence my degree. When I arrived there, I would have to inform my relatives, arrange the temple for the wedding, hand out invitations and organise the wedding while handling family dynamics and getting married within a very tight timeframe.

I thought of Krish and his support throughout the years. I am sure he would have liked to be present at my wedding, but he would have insisted everything to go his way and I was not prepared to let that happen. So after some serious deliberations, I decided not to inform my older brother about my wedding plans. He would have objected to them anyway, and I was not prepared to face additional stress, so it was best that I inform him of my plans later.

I was equally concerned about my other family members, to whom I had not told about my marriage. I thought about it several times and decided not to inform them of my plans until I arrived in Malaysia. I was aware that my families would be disappointed when they heard about my decision to marry someone outside our caste, but their support would remain the same. To minimise their stressful duration, I informed my mother, Mano and Jaya in Malaysia about my wedding after I had booked my plane ticket.

< 7 >   The freedom to make my own decisions

My three-week itinerary for Malaysia was to finalise the wedding arrangements in the first week, proceed with the wedding in the second week and return to UK in the third week.

On the day of my flight, I began to worry about my professional status and my poor financial position. Those two issues would be a concern for any reasonable mother-in-law. As I was only about to commence my tertiary study, there was no guarantee that I would finish the degree successfully. At the same time, my bank account balance was so bad that I could not have paid for even a simple wedding, but the decision to get married was mine, so I did not want to ask help from anyone for cash. Suba and I discussed and agreed to keep the temple wedding simple, and to be blessed by Suba's mother and mine, as they were both widows.

Being absorbed in my own worries, I did not realise that the plane was well on its way and the noise from the in-flight drink service caught my attention. Not long after, I began enjoying the in-flight service and imbibing the alcohol slowly. After a few shots of whisky, my anxiety level slowly faded away and I fell asleep.

The next time I opened my eyes was when I heard the announcement for dinner. Again, there was a small bottle of wine with my food. I felt a bit tipsy and did not want any further alcohol, but instead read the in-flight magazines until I reached Kuala Lumpur International Airport. It was just after midnight when the plane touched down. I felt nervous when I thought of the people I was going to meet at the airport, especially my unmet future in-laws. One person that would be familiar at the arrival terminal was my future wife; I was really looking forward to seeing Suba again and finding out how she had gone organising some of the wedding plans (although I found out later that nothing had been done). By the time I collected my luggage and made my way to the airport exit, it was nearly 1.00am.

As I pushed my trolley and exited the air-conditioned venue, I felt the Malaysian heat and humidity. I had to remove my jacket and necktie and start wiping my face. Except for the humidity, I felt a little drunk but relaxed; I started smiling and became talkative. I was also concerned that my future in-laws' first impression of me be very positive. When Suba first greeted me, she sensed that I had a bit too much to drink, but she saw I was controlling myself well. Suba's younger brother, Rajeevan (Raji), was there to greet me as well. Soon, I was escorted to Raji's car with my luggage to go to Suba's house and meet her mother and family.

During the thirty-minute journey from the airport to Suba's house, the conversation in the car was very monotonous. I was responding to questions about living in UK, the weather and my flight. I did not get a chance to speak privately with Suba, and when we spoke, we kept our conversation formal. We only had one close hug as I came out of the airport. Even in the car we did not hold hands, as it was not the custom. We were controlling our emotions as much as we could; we wanted to hug and talk to each other in private, but it was impossible. It was difficult for us to restrict ourselves to formal conversation with each other as we hadn't seen each other for six months. Even though we were close now, we felt so far apart.

< 7 >   The freedom to make my own decisions

As the car pulled in at Suba's house, I was greeted by Suba's mother and her brother Suresh and cousin Sunitha. My future mother-in-law was pleased to see me and welcomed me into the house, unlike Raji, who immediately disappeared to do his personal work. I quickly found my way around the house and had a refreshing cold shower before changing into my pyjamas.

By the time I had changed, Suba's mother had heated my dinner for me and said that she had been waiting to have dinner with me. I felt that she cared for me as I would soon be her son-in-law. Although I have had the food and drinks in the plane, I did not want to disappoint her, so I accepted her invitation for another big meal!

By the time we were seated for the dinner she had specially prepared for my arrival, it was already 2.00am. She had a lot of questions to ask. She did not ask about my job at the time, possibly because Suba had already mentioned it to her, but I quickly updated her about my friendship with Suba and how it had developed into a serious relationship. She was happy when I showed her the photos of us taken during our courtship in Scotland. I also explained to her that I was about to commence my degree at the end of that year, after the wedding. She was happy to know that I had worked as an Registered Nurse to save some money over the last few months before coming to Malaysia. She explained how her life had changed since she had lost her husband. I acknowledged her sorrow; her story reminded me of my own mother's situation, and how she had to cope through difficult times without a husband.

As we ate and talked, our formality slowly disappeared,

and we were comfortable sharing our views freely without any hesitation. She commented that I had a good appetite, just like her late husband, which made me feel great. By the time we finished our meals and conversation, I noticed that the rest of the family had gone to sleep. As the flight fatigue crept up on me and my eyes began closing, we decided to finish our chat as it was almost 4.00am.

In bed, I thought of Suba's family and how all of them had been very warm towards me, except for Raji. Since the airport, his body language had indicated he was not accepting me warmly. I guess he thought I was not a worthy husband for his sister as I did not draw a good income like him. At the time, he was earning a huge income from his full-time work with contract positions in the building industry. He had a continental car and was able to pay his expenses, whereas I was barely surviving.

He was also frustrated with his sister and how she had fallen in love with me. He was puzzled as to why on earth she wanted to marry a poor, non-professional person, despite all the great proposals she'd had in the past.

I analysed that there were some marked differences between how we saw the world. His world was very materialistic, whereas mine was about people and their connections. As the breadwinner of the family, he was caring for his mother, younger brother and cousin, as well as ensuring their education and welfare, which I admired. Due to these commitments, he had to be very materialistic and often talked about people's income and wealth. Obviously, he did not see any common interests between us. It must have frustrated

< 7 > The freedom to make my own decisions

him because I would soon be his brother-in-law and would not meet his expectations. Unfortunately, my journey was very different to his, which he did not know, and his snappy, hurtful remarks continued throughout my stay in Malaysia.

After a good sleep, I was refreshed and ready for a home-cooked breakfast. Suba's mother listened attentively to my childhood story and showed empathy when I mentioned that I had lost my dad at the age of four. She impressed upon me the fact that she was proud of her children and loved them all dearly. She also commented how Suba, being the only girl in the family, had been spoilt, and had never listened to anyone in the family. She had done whatever she wanted to do, her way, but she was a very studious girl. Soon after her "O" Levels, she had pestered her parents to send her overseas for nursing. As her father's favourite, she was allowed to study abroad.

Soon after breakfast, I said 'Hello' to Suresh and Sunitha. Suresh was eleven years old and in Form III, while his cousin, Sunitha, was seven and in Primary 4. After speaking with them, I understood they were very different. As the youngest in the family, Sunitha was the darling of the family. I was informed by Suba's mum that she was adopted when her biological mother, Suba's maternal aunt had passed away giving birth. Sunitha was brought up by Suba's mother like her own child and had been pampered since childhood because she was a "motherless" child. One afternoon, I was surprised to see Suba's mother hand-feeding her lunch at the age of seven. In the mornings she had to wake Sunitha and help her shower and dress her before she went to school. Suba's mum had promised her younger sister that she would care for her child and felt obliged to do so, but to me her caring had become pampering. As Suba's mum was not working, she had the time for Sunitha, and as Suba had moved overseas, Sunitha became the substitute daughter.

On the other hand, Suresh was very quiet, with low self-esteem. Although he knew that I would soon be his brother-in-law, he still found it difficult to talk to me. Suba confirmed my observation of Sunitha and Suresh and their ongoing sibling rivalry. Part of the rivalry was caused by the attention given to Sunitha, who had taken the place as the youngest in the family. Sunitha had also become Raji's favourite. I noticed that when Raji got home, he often spent time with Sunitha, but not with Suresh, who anticipated the same attention but was denied any. When Raji had free time, he took Sunitha for a ride, but left Suresh out.

Unlike Suresh, Sunitha was much more alert and confident with a charming personality. She spoke better English than Suresh despite being four years younger. Sunitha often earned Raji's praises on small tasks, such as taking telephone messages. When Sunitha answered phone calls, she took detailed notes about the caller, while Suresh often failed do that and therefore he was not praised but told to improve himself.

I suppose my mother-in-law-to-be did not seriously consider the growing rivalry between Suresh and Sunitha.

‹ 8 ›

The unforgettable Hindu wedding

Most conversations in Suba's house after my arrival were about the wedding. As I grew closer to my future mother-in-law, she began to share some of her concerns about Suba's outfits. Suba often dressed in short pants with a light cotton top because of the hot and humid Malaysian weather. Suba's mother was not happy with this because she was concerned about what the neighbours might think or gossip to each other. According to Suba's mother, convenience and comfortable dressing was not as important as the traditional Indian neighbours' perception of the bride-to-be. She had expected Suba to be in traditional Indian dress with a long skirt or sari, especially as she was about to be married. Unfortunately, Suba did what she thought was most practical and ignored the opinions of others.

After a few days of relaxing at Suba's place, I realised that my plans of breaking my wedding news to my family (who didn't live in KL), the temple reservation, the printing of invitation cards, catering for the wedding and the purchase of the wedding sari all needed to be done in the next two weeks.

I had been warned that most temples would be fully booked because we were in the popular season for Hindu weddings. My initial task was to ensure a temple was booked as early as possible. Fortunately, Suba's older brother (Faisal) was working in Malaysia as a Civil Engineer at that time and said he was available to provide transport. I gladly took his offer and he drove Suba and me to the temple closest to their place. The Kajang Murugan Temple, apart from being away from the central business district of KL, also had sufficient parking for guests. According to the priest, we were very lucky to book the only available day for the next fortnight.

The priest said the traditional wedding protocols of the ceremony could take a long time, but he promised us to keep the wedding short. Suba and I were glad of the priest's command of English, as my Tamil was rusty. We explained to him that we had to return to UK soon after the wedding and we would be formally married through the Malaysian Registry before the temple ceremony. He also understood that our primary reason for a second wedding in a temple was for the two families, in particular for the two widowed mothers. We wanted them to witness the wedding because Suba was the only girl in her family, and I was the last child to get married in my family. Before we left, the priest summarised the wedding protocol and agreed to keep the ceremony short and to complete all the wedding rituals within three hours. Suba and I were relieved to have booked a very cooperative priest.

< 8 > The unforgettable Hindu wedding

In Malaysia, Hindu weddings are commonly held in temples because they are considered sacred places for holy matrimonies and follow strict protocols. Shoes had to be removed and feet washed as people entered the temple, with water often available at the temple entrance. All food at the temple had to be vegetarian and no outside food could be brought into the temple grounds without permission. Only religious or devotional music could be played, and no one was allowed to be too close to the Hindu idols except the priests. No activity was permitted in the temple grounds without the priest's approval. On the chosen day, our wedding was the only function taking place at the temple.

When we explained the temple arrangement to Suba's mother, she was glad to know that we had chosen her regular place of worship for the wedding. We were aware that we would not have many wedding guests because we had not informed them well in advance. Wedding cards are the usual formal invitations to any Hindu wedding. We had not even printed the cards yet and our wedding date was only two weeks away, so we didn't have much time to print and distribute the cards. I was not happy with the short notice for my guests, but that was my situation at that time. Luckily, many of the guests we planned to invite were family members who understood our circumstances and were glad to acknowledge that we were attempting the process in a respectful manner with printed cards, even if there wasn't much notice.

The wedding cards were printed with Raji's help. Raji had good friends in the printing industry and promised to get it done within seven days following our drafted copy. As the printers deal with many of wedding cards in their daily business, they did not need much input on what to put on the cards. Suba and I agreed the words should be written in Tamil and English. Many of my relatives were comfortable reading Tamil, but not English. We only requested sixty cards because we did not have time to invite all our friends, and we also did know their addresses. Given the very short notice, we were uncertain as to how many of them would turn up.

As soon as the cards were printed, I visited my immediate family members to distribute them. Firstly, I visited my mother, next was my brother Mano, followed by several uncles and then a few extended families that lived further away.

I did not impose on any of my relatives for help, nor Suba's family, but decided to find my own way to distribute the cards using public transport. I was aware that my journey would take a few hours because of the distance between the states in Malaysia.

As I was travelling, I recalled the journey I had undertaken twelve years ago when I was fifteen. Rapid developments had taken place in Malaysia over those years. Much of the land along the highway was now housing estates. The new housing estate developers had removed the virgin hills and mountains and replaced them with concrete buildings with two-three-storey houses. There were large signboards showing the prices of the properties for sale, and I wondered if the poor people could afford these lovely-looking properties.

The comfortable coach trip took about three-and-a-half hours on the new highway. The coach now had cushioned seats and air-conditioning. In 1963, when I had last travelled

< 8 > The unforgettable Hindu wedding

the journey was tiring because of the solid plastic seats with no cushioning or back rests. Sometimes the whole coach would shake when its wheels went over any bumps, but with the improved roads and better wheels, the ride was much smoother this time.

As I was on my way to see my second sister Jaya, I remembered the times when I lived with her family. They had moved to a place called Kuala Kangsar (KK) which was my birthplace and a royal town in Malaysia. All three of their children had left home. At the time of my wedding, her two daughters were working in KL, while her son was studying in the UK. My sister and her husband lived happily in their own timber house. They grew their own crops in a vegetable patch at the back of the house where they harvested enough for their own needs. Sometimes when their garden yield exceeded their needs, my sister bartered with her neighbours for different vegetables.

They also owned a few acres of rubber plantation where they worked seven days a week. They tapped the rubber trees for the latex, which was collected and coagulated before being made into sheets. The sheets were dried before they were sold. The income from tapping the trees covered their living expenses.

When I met them, they acknowledged that the plantation work was exhausting, but they were happy because they were not accountable to anyone. As they owned the small holding, they could stay off from work on rainy days or if they did not feel well. They also enjoyed the flexibility of going away to visit relatives during the endless rainy monsoon seasons.

They had been extremely helpful during my school days. At one stage they were even prepared to sell their only property to pay for my fees to study medicine in India. Despite their poor circumstances, they had never denied me love and care and they were prepared to help me at any cost. They were very fond of me and had expectations that I would marry one of their daughters in the future, which is a traditionally accepted Hindu practice. I had no intention of marrying any of my nieces because I had looked after them when they were babies. I also now realised that marriages within families had high possibilities of congenital birth defects. Perhaps, if I had not gone overseas, and studied nursing and broadened my knowledge, I would have followed their expectations and married one of their daughters.

I was terrified to break the news to them as they would be heartbroken. The last thing I wanted was to hurt them, but I had no choice. As I broke the news to both of them, there was an intense emotional moment between all of us. They were in tears when they heard of my forthcoming wedding and I was in tears to see them upset. Despite my disappointing message, they didn't say anything negative but reassured me instead. It just showed that their love and support for me hadn't diminished despite news of my marriage. Following the upsetting news and their emotional state, it was equally difficult for me to update them with the progress of my wedding plans.

Somehow, I managed to explain to them how Suba and I had got to know each other over the years and how I had recently met the rest of her family. Both my sister and her

< 8 > The unforgettable Hindu wedding

husband accepted my explanation, but they were concerned about how I was going to manage the wedding expenses. I explained to them that I did not have much cash, so the temple wedding had to be very simple and the bride's family, aware of my situation, would pay for the expenses. I explained that as the groom-to-be, I had managed to get a wedding ring and sari for the bride. Again, despite hearing my upsetting news, they still insisted on making earrings and a *thali* (a type of necklace) for the bride as a gift. Initially, I did not want to accept their present, but then my sister explained that it was a customary practice in Hindu culture for the groom's family to offer the *thali*. Their contribution definitely eased another cost for the wedding.

As I was heading to the next stopover, I was thinking about the *thali*. In Hindu culture it is normally the parents who do the *thali* for their child's wedding. In my case, my sister and her husband saw me more like a son, as I had spent considerable years under their care. It assured me that their love had not perished, despite their disappointment at me not marrying one of their daughters.

After the sad and stressful day at my sister's place, I visited my third brother Mano and his family, who lived an hour away from my sister's place. Mano was also surprised with my decision to marry outside our family as he had also expected that I would marry one of our nieces. He had a lot of questions about how well I knew Suba and her family. I was not perturbed by his concerns because those kinds of questions were expected from the groom's elders.

It was the first time I had noticed how well his basic,

three-bedroom brick veneer suited his family of four (he now had a son and daughter). They also had a small garden to grow their own vegetables. He did not offer any financial help, but I had not expected anything from him. He had not completed his secondary school, but luckily his government position included paid sick days and a pension until his death. He shared his regrets for not completing his secondary education as that would have helped him earn a better income.

After Mano's house, I left for my uncle's place. He was my father's stepbrother and had seldom visited us. I had not visited him for more than twenty years and I only had a vague idea of where he lived. I remembered he had the gift of the gab, telling jokes to the crowd that often gathered around him at functions and parties.

By the time I arrived at his village, it was dusk. I had to ask several people as I searched for his place, and when I finally got there, he and his wife were away. I had no choice but to hand over the wedding card to his neighbour, who kindly accepted it on his behalf and escorted me back to the bus stop for my safe return to my sister's house in KK.

The next day, I returned to KL to visit my brother, Maniam. He had retired early from the Malaysian Territorial Army where he had served as a Warrant Officer, and lived by himself. His four children were all married and lived by themselves with their families. He had also married outside the culture and understood the issues grooms had to face when marrying a person outside their caste.

He had few questions about my wedding and was upfront about being unable to offer any financial support, although

< 8 > The unforgettable Hindu wedding

he did offer moral support. I was pleased to have his support, and I was reminded how unlike Krish, Maniam was.

As I was in KL, I also delivered the wedding invitation to my oldest sister, Saras. She was pleasantly surprised to see me appear unannounced. She had two boys and six girls, all of whom were working, except for her youngest son who was an undergraduate at the local Malaysian university. Saras was very fond of me because I looked very much like my dad and was the baby of the family. She was excited about the news she had already heard through the local family network. She would have been happier if I had married one of her daughters, but again I expressed my reasons for not marrying one of my nieces. My sister's mother-in-law was also very affectionate towards me. She was equally excited to hear of my wedding, especially that I had found a girl outside of my family. The next questions were expected: how old was Suba, what was her family background, her education, her occupation. As the youngest brother, I had no choice but to answer.

My sister was also pleased to hear that I had been accepted into Aberdeen University and would commence my study on my return to the UK She warned me that not all her children could attend the wedding because most of her daughters did shift work. I also knew she did not have her own vehicle and it would be an effort to attend. I did not pressure my sister's family to attend my wedding but allowed her to decide whatever was manageable for them. They were delighted that I understood about their constraints if they were compelled to attend. I was very pleased that Saras and her husband promised to attend the wedding. She hugged me and blessed me before I left her place.

The one other important person who had helped me was my oldest brother, Krish. Despite his authoritative nature, he had an interest in my future, but did not know how to convey it in a non-demanding way. As he was still working in UK at the time, I had not communicated with him for months prior to the wedding, I was glad to post him a card to get his blessings rather than facing him in person.

On my return to Suba's place, her mother reminded me that it was customary to hand-deliver wedding cards personally to their close elderly relatives and to get their blessings before the wedding. Although Suba's mother knew many of those elders may not be in a position to attend the wedding, it was customary that they should still be invited. I followed Faisal to deliver the cards to their elderly relatives who lived far away.

I was exploring how to get through my wedding day without purchasing a wedding garment. As my time was limited, I was not able to get one sewn nor even have time to shop for one. I was prepared to wear the pants and jacket I had worn on my journey from UK. Unfortunately, according to the Indian tradition, the groom was expected to wear something culturally appropriate for the wedding because it's a very special day and was held in a temple.

I had accidentally enquired about Mano's wedding attire when I visited him. When he showed it to me, I was very pleased to note that his size was similar to mine, although he was slightly shorter than me. He knew it was not accepted practice to wear someone else's wedding attire, but we both promised not to share the secret until the wedding was over. He promised me that he would get it laundered and bring it to the temple on my wedding day. I felt quite relieved to have traditional attire rather than shirt and pants.

I was also concerned about Suba's wedding attire, as she would be the centre of attention on the day. I knew I had to buy the wedding sari for her, but I did not know anyone who was going to assist me in the few free days I had prior to the wedding. Luckily, my aunty was familiar with my requirements and knew my financial position, so she offered to help me to purchase them within my budget. My mother-in-law-to-be was very pleased to see the purchased bridal items were of good quality, even though I was facing financial difficulties.

Prior to the wedding, I had made it clear to my mother-in-law that I would not be able to buy any wedding clothes for the family. She was very happy for my honesty about my financial circumstances. If I had been wealthy, I would have planned the wedding in advance and purchased all of the wedding attire for all my relatives. I was lucky to have enough money for Suba's wedding sari.

On the same afternoon, I ordered wedding garlands within my price range from the florists. I remembered that someone had warned me it was difficult to purchase fresh flowers during the Malaysian dry season, but I was lucky to pick up the flowers freshly arranged on the morning of the wedding.

Generally, at Hindu weddings the groom's house was busy, but we did not have a "family home". All six members of my family had dispersed and did not really live under one roof, and

I was in no position to purchase a house myself. My mother, who stayed with my sisters for no more than six months at a time, did not need a permanent residence. My oldest sister's children and in-laws lived in her husband's home, but it was far away from the temple. Jaya had her own house which was also far from the temple. There was no home convenient for my guests, except my uncle's house. My Uncle Rama was my step-grandmother's son. When my father's biological mother passed away from illness, my grandfather had remarried. My grandfather had two sons from his second marriage, one of whom was Rama. I only came to know him when I was starting secondary school.

Although his two-bedroom house was not a large place, it served my purpose at this time when I did not have many options to choose from. It must have been quite inconvenient for my uncle's family, but they were very supportive as they understood my circumstances. They had often welcomed me when I dropped in for a day or two during my younger days. Prior to the wedding, I had shared my wedding plans, which made them feel included and therefore prepared to put up with a disruption to their routine. Their only son (Raja) was around eighteen years old and was very helpful to Suba and me at the wedding.

When I met my mother for the first time since returning to Malaysia, I was surprised to notice that she had aged and that her memory was not as good as before. Recalling the scene at the airport and how she had cried pointing to the plane when I was about to take off, I was in tears when I saw her at my uncle's place. I told her Suba's background briefly and

< 8 > The unforgettable Hindu wedding

explained to her that the girl I was about to marry would be a stranger to all of us. When I mentioned that Suba came from a different sub-culture and did not speak the same language as her, I noticed how my mother had mellowed a lot about her caste. She did not utter any objections when I broke the news. She was very happy to see me return to Malaysia to get married in her presence.

My mother had missed her eldest son's wedding as he had got married in the UK and so my wedding would be a special one for her, as I was the youngest child and she felt happy to be able to witness my marriage. From a cultural perspective, the number-six child's wedding should be the most grandly celebrated marriage. I presumed she must have had grand plans on how she would have liked me to be married, but our family circumstances had changed following my father's death.

A few days before the wedding, I took my mother to visit Suba's mother so that they would be acquainted before becoming in-laws. It was not easy for them to start talking when they first met. It was quite strange as my mother had never eaten in other people's houses or mixed with people unless they were related or had known to her for a while. I remember when a cup of tea was offered to her at Suba's place, she found it difficult to drink. I had to insist that it was alright as we were going to be relatives. At the meeting, my mother was quite uncertain about what questions to ask because she was not involved in any part of the wedding discussions or arrangements. My mum, in the old Indian mentality, had expected to receive a huge dowry as the groom's mother. I made it very clear to both of them that the wedding would take place without any exchange of cash or jewellery between the families. I emphasised these points very clearly in Tamil so that both of them understood.

My wedding situation was a race against time while trying to keep my family calm. They hadn't received much notice and it was unorthodox not to give them the opportunity to provide input. Because of the short time frame, we had to be willing to compromise. The night before the wedding I went with my mother and stayed at Suba's mother's house, while Suba stayed at Faisal, her oldest brother's place. As part of Indian custom, the bride and groom stayed in separate homes until they were officially married. Suba's mother gladly received both of us that night. It was great to see my mother and Suba's mother having dinner together before my mother retired to bed. I stayed back and talked to Suba's mother, who was waiting for the opportunity. She expressed how happy she was that Suba was getting married. She was also sad to say that she would miss her after the wedding as we had to return to Scotland. She also shared how Suba was the only girl in the family and a daddy's girl who got away with a lot of mischief. My future mother-in-law also asked for forgiveness from me if Suba was to be unreasonable and became argumentative. I was blown away with her frank, open and humble words.

She had also observed how Suba was very stubborn and had her way in small decisions between the two of us. She had noticed and heard Suba's remarks to me, which, in her opinion, were very harsh at times with an inappropriate tone. I reassured her that Suba and I would work through our differences after our wedding. I felt very sorry for her because Suba had a mind of her own and never hesitated to express her thoughts her thoughts even if they were different from that of her mother's. I had noticed her behavior in the short time I had spent with them in Malaysia.

Our conversation continued into the night as Suba's mother told me her family stories. She expressed her concern about Suresh and Sunitha. She was worried about what might happen to them if she was debilitated or suddenly passed away.

I was not sure what to say when I noticed her sad face and teary eyes, but I promised her that I would help them as best I could. As I was very uncertain about my own future at that time, I was unable to make definite promises. I knew that Suba's older brother was working as an engineer, and in his very comfortable position he did not expect any support for Suresh and Sunitha from me. By the time we finished our conversation, it was three in the morning on my wedding day!

I managed to sleep for a couple of hours, but was not sure whether my mother-in-law had slept at all that night. I was up at 6.00am, and was dreaming of the day I would be back in Scotland in my routine with all these hassles behind me, but today I had to focus because it was a very special day in my life!

Suba's mother was glad to know that her temple of worship had been chosen for the wedding ceremony and she was briefed that we would follow the traditional wedding process under the guidance of the priest. We were aware that our guests would not realise we were having a shorter wedding ceremony.

The wedding would be in an Indian temple about five kilometres from Suba's house at 3.00pm. We were expecting around one hundred guests, mainly relatives and a few very close friends. The guests were expected to attend the ceremony and reception, which was to be held in the same temple. Faisal had arranged one of his friend's cars to be the official "wedding car" to transport the bride and groom.

My wedding day did not finish without its challenges, which I had expected, especially because two sub-cultures were involved. Soon after I woke up, I had a surprising request from my mother-in-law. She wanted me to fast because she had taken a vow that I would fast till the marriage ceremony was over. According to my mother-in-law, the fasting would remove future hurdles for the newlywed couple. As this was a small request and it would not cost me anything, I agreed to abstain from eating on my wedding day until the ceremony was over. I did not realise the next surprise waiting for me from my mother!

My mother always had a habit of hand-feeding me when I was around her and she had done this ever since my primary school days. She had missed me a lot when our family separated after my father's death and she knew that I would be going away soon after the wedding. On my wedding day, she had watched me busy making last minute arrangements around the house as she was eating her lunch, and she could not resist her old habit of showing her affection by feeding me. She waved to me to come over to her. I was in a dilemma. I was not sure what the right thing to do was: should I refuse my mother's wish and let her know that I had just promised my mother-in-law I would only eat when the wedding reception was over? Initially, I pretended that I did not notice her, but I knew she would not let it go. Seeing her waiting for me, I did not have the courage to refuse her showing her love and affection towards me, as it was also a special day for her. All she wanted was to feed me. I realised that day I would be married soon and far away from her, and I did not want to miss the last opportunity to indulge my mother's small request.

I quickly looked around to ensure that my mother-in-law was not in sight and accepted my mother's food. I saw her happiness as she was feeding me, a priceless moment of my mother's love that I still cherish now. After three mouthfuls of my mother's feeding, I quickly ran into the bathroom to ensure that I had no food on my face just in case my mother-in-law noticed it.

By then I was full and re-energised for the remainder of the Big Day. I thanked my Lord Ganesha for the moment with my mother and also asked for his forgiveness for betraying my mother-in-law. To this day, I sometimes feel guilty about what I did, but at the same time I could not say no to my mother's simple request.

I was glad to escape the first challenge, but did not know a second hurdle was waiting for me. Just like any wedding house, Suba's house was overflowing with visitors and relatives and there hadn't been enough time for them all to be introduced. In the midst of the busy crowd, I sensed something had gone wrong when I noticed my brother Mano crying. Soon after that, I noticed my sister Jaya, was also upset and wiping her tears. When I saw my siblings in tears just before the wedding, I did not know what I should do. I knew they weren't sad because of the wedding as I had their blessings, so something must have happened.

When I asked my sister why my brother was in tears, she mentioned that she had been equally upset to hear Raji's condemning remarks about me to some of his friends and relatives. Mano was very angry about Raji's remarks and was ready to pull him up in public to embarrass him. I warned my brother that this would only add fuel to the fire and also tarnish our family's reputation. Not long after this, Faisal's wife, Arnie, also shared that She had found Raji's remarks about me disturbing. Arnie felt sorry that my siblings had heard such remarks as she knew they were only visiting Suba's house because of my wedding. I felt sorry that they had to hear his cruel remarks because of me. I knew he was very capable of upsetting anyone with his arrogant behaviour. I was angry and helpless and did not know what to do but to calm the three worried people. I asked them not to get upset because Suba and I would be gone from the house soon after the wedding.

I was already tense with the commotion created by Raji. My relatives were very simple people and they had come to show their love and support at my wedding. They were not wealthy but they were very fond of me and they all loved me for what I had achieved so far. They had every right to be hurt by unfair remarks about me from anyone. Fortunately, they did not say a word to Raji and instead, ignored him!

As the wedding was approaching, I went to the temple for the first part of the ritual dressed in Indian attire: a white shirt with a white *vesti* (a loose cloth wrapped around the waist

< 8 > The unforgettable Hindu wedding

that hangs from the hip to the toes). The simple dress code did not perturb me, as after the first ritual I was prepared to be dressed again to come back for the second and final part of the ceremony, seated next to Suba. My second outfit lifted my appearance as a groom because my brother's wedding gear fitted me perfectly.

Suba's behaviour at the wedding remained unchanged and some of my relatives began to doubt whether she was the most suitable wife for me. Their doubts were based on seeing the difference in our behaviour. My relatives knew I was brought up very reserved and had learned to be humble and respectful towards elders. I would not argue with anyone if it hurt the other person, and I had been taught to earn the respect of our people and community. However, Suba had a distinct personality and did what she thought was correct, irrespective of people's feelings and their views. Even on our wedding day, I felt I had to go along with her, as she wanted to lead. There were times I felt hurt on our wedding day as she was not willing to see things from my perspective or to even hear my views. I felt Raji had total control over her and she did whatever he wanted, but not what I, her future husband, would have liked. I knew I did not have the support of my wife to-be, but I controlled myself and hoped that things would sort out when we returned to Scotland.

At the wedding, we were seated in front of about one hundred guests and I did not imagine what they were about to witness. As the wedding went on, I quietly reminded the priest to proceed as quickly as possible. Meanwhile, my assigned best man, Raji, who was standing next to me for the first twenty minutes of the wedding rituals, suddenly disappeared from the scene. I looked for him in the crowd, but could not see him.

I was shocked at what he had done to me. Faisal, who was watching my nervous expression, came forward and calmed me down saying that he would take the place of the best man. I felt very strange and angry, but was left with no choice. I had to remain calm as the crowd's eyes were focused on me. I pretended to be enjoying my big day and smiled despite my anger and frustration. I felt what he had done was absolutely unacceptable, especially on his only sister's wedding day.

As the wedding progressed, I did not expect that there was another disaster waiting for me! The surprise came when we had to exchange wedding rings. I whispered to Suba for the wedding ring she should have brought with her. The priest prolonged the ritual with the hope the ring would turn up, but Suba gave me a blank look and said she did not have it with her. I was very disappointed with her because I had reminded her to bring the ring without fail, several times, prior to the wedding. My tension was rising, but I resolved to appear calm.

Our guests must have wondered why there was a delay in the otherwise swiftly progressing ceremony. Faisal was standing next to me, so I quickly asked him to slip his wedding ring into my hand. He managed to pass it to me discreetly and I passed onto the priest. The priest was very understanding and carried on with the ceremony without pause. I managed to appear calm and show no reaction to the disasters that were upsetting me.

All of these challenges were very hurtful. I was very surprised by my future wife's behaviour and why she was acting so differently. When we had been in Scotland, she was very supportive and often shared my views. Unfortunately, her behaviour had completely changed after her six months in Malaysia. She began to disagree with almost anything I suggested, and sometimes her comments were very hurtful and abrupt. She was very demanding and she did not want to compromise. I always had to give in to keep the situation between us calm. I felt that I had made a big mistake and had been blinded by love; I was worried I was seeing the real Suba now. In short, I was not a happy man at my wedding. Several of my relatives who knew me well noticed that I was not happy during the ceremony. With all these thoughts crossing my mind, I was asking why I had to put up with these hassles, and if it was going to be worth it. For a moment I even thought of calling off the wedding.

Fortunately, I was distracted from my serious thoughts by the priest. He kept the ceremony going and wanted me to pay full attention as people were watching us because we both were the centre of attention. Fortunately, the ceremony came to an end after two hours and I finally felt relaxed, but I still was not sure whether I had done the right thing.

‹ 9 ›

Unexpected hurdles after my wedding

As soon as the ceremony finished, I came to meet the crowd and thanked them for attending. Many members of Suba's family spoke in Malayalam, while I spoke in Tamil. The usual questions from the guests were about my job and what living in Scotland was like. When we spoke later, Suba said she had been asked the same questions by my family, and we had responded similarly. Soon afterwards my mother and mother-in-law invited everyone to join them for a light meal at the temple, as was the custom.

I certainly enjoyed the food as I had hardly eaten anything that day, other than the three mouthfuls of food from my mother that morning. As soon as I finished my meal, I joined the guests again to say goodbye. I had not seen some of them for several years and we were excited to see each other. I also had to say goodbye to my mother because I was returning to Scotland in a few days. I wanted to see her before I left Malaysia, but, unfortunately, circumstances did not permit it.

It was quite sad saying goodbye to my mother because I

< 9 > Unexpected hurdles after my wedding

knew that within minutes of the wedding ending, she would be missing me, and I knew that my close family would be equally sad. Before they left the temple, I spent some time explaining my situation and I promised to return to Malaysia when my education and employment were sorted out.

By the time I had said goodbye to all the guests, more than three hours had passed since the wedding had ended. As the wedding car was waiting to fetch my new bride and me, I had to quickly end my conversations.

The usual Indian custom was to bring the newly-wedded wife to the groom's home, but given our situation, Faisal graciously hosted us. After a cold shower, I quickly changed into my usual sarong (a cylindrical cloth worn round the waist), while Suba donned her kaftan.

Even after the wedding, I still felt that Suba was disconnected. Her dismissive behaviour continued the day after our wedding. I expected her to show some affection towards me or at least pretend to do so as my new wife! Instead, she was quite cold. I wondered whether I had made a big mistake. I also wondered whether her behaviour was related to the realisation that I was poor. I felt lonely at Faisal's house, and sad that I had disappointed my family by marrying an unknown girl. When we were at Faisal's place, she was fully engaged in conversation with her family and friends, while I was the quiet listener. On our wedding night, I had very few words with her. In fact, I had more conversation with Faisal's family than Suba. It was Arnie (Faisal's wife) who asked me if I needed a drink or something to eat, while Suba was too absorbed with herself. I went to bed around 11.00pm that night, while Suba was still talking with her sister-in-law until the early hours of the morning.

The next day, I woke up around 7.30am and was very surprised to find that my new wife had breakfast with her brother and sister-in-law. I was not at all concerned that she had breakfast already, but the fact that she did not have the courtesy to call me to join her was hurtful. I did not understand why she did not make the small effort to invite me for a later breakfast. I could not follow her logic. I was certain that she was not so hungry that she could not have waited. I felt we had missed an opportunity for our first meal together as husband and wife.

Again, things were flashing in my brain and I was questioning her strange behaviour. The love she had shown me when we were courting for five years in Scotland seemed to have disappeared. I wondered if she had married me so that I would take orders from her and do as I was told. I was very puzzled and unsure whether I had done the right thing in getting married. I prayed to my dad and hoped everything would work out.

I was still miserable the afternoon after my wedding. All the commotion that had happened prior to my wedding was still fresh in my mind. I was very uncomfortable with Suba's continued behaviour. All of my relatives had left Suba's place in an unhappy mood because of Raji's remarks. He had disliked me from the moment I had landed in Malaysia and had caused enough discomfort for my family and me. As I did not have the support I had expected from my new wife, I decided to return to Scotland as soon as possible. When I

< 9 >   Unexpected hurdles after my wedding

explained to Suba that I wanted to return as I had things to do before university commenced, she surprisingly agreed without any questions.

My trip home quickly became complicated. Three days after my wedding, I rang the travel agent and presented our travel tickets for an earlier return flight to UK. She called later that evening to say that there were no seats on any return flights but she had listed our names in case a standby flight became available.

Later, I realised I had gone to the wrong travel agent because she was a very good friend of Raji. The next morning, she called me to say that she had found a vacant seat for one person on a direct flight from KL to London via Bangkok. The second seat was only available from KL to Bangkok, but passengers had to wait in Bangkok until midnight to connect to the London flight. I had no choice but to get on that flight and wait in Bangkok for Suba's connection. When I agreed to the agent's conditions, I didn't realise that the flight was that day, that afternoon.

Once again, my race against time had started. Luckily, Suba and I had packed luggage already as we were on the waiting list. I, somehow, had to get to the airport on time. I knew that getting there from Suba's house was not just about the forty-kilometre trip, but also the traffic in KL. When I received the call that morning, it was 10.00am and the flight was scheduled for 1.00pm. Boarding for the flight would start at least an hour before the scheduled take-off time. As the flight was scheduled to depart at 1.00pm, I had to be at the international airport check-in point by midday. I still had my doubts as to whether it was worth taking the chance, but I had no other alternative for an early return. I was upset we were not returning together as a couple. Leaving my new wife behind was the last thing I had ever thought of but I was in a difficult situation. Luckily, when I called the agent to discuss the flight, my cousin, Raj, overheard my conversation and nodded, telling me to go ahead and to take the chance.

Raj was reliable and had been helpful at my wedding. He was my Uncle Rama's son, and his house had been used as a base for my wedding. I was impressed with his sensitivity when he overheard my problems and offered to help me. Raj was confident that we could make it to the airport on time on his new motorbike that he had purchased only a few months earlier. He felt that my situation was a great opportunity to test his motorbike's speed capacity. He said he was happy to help, but warned me that I had to be ready to leave in no more than thirty minutes. I ensured that I had all of my travel documents and that I was ready to leave the house by 10.30am after a quick goodbye to everyone at the house. As it was impossible to carry more than one small piece of luggage with me on the bike, I left my larger bag for Suba to bring along. I was focused on reaching the airport on time. I did not have much time to say goodbye to Suba, but she assured me that she would be on the flight that I would be reboarding in Bangkok around midnight.

Raj was confident he could get me to the airport on time as he knew the roads of KL quite well, including all of the one-way roads. I held him tight as we weaved through the waiting vehicles to get to the front of the queue whenever we were

< 9 > Unexpected hurdles after my wedding

stopped at the traffic lights. He definitely broke the speed limit as he flew past traffic to get me to the airport on time.

I saw the relief on Raj's face when we finally reached the airport just before midday. As I got off the bike, I quickly hugged him and thanked him before heading to the ticket counter. I had fifty minutes left before the boarding gates would shut. The check-in reception staff advised me to quickly get to the customs clearance area before I missed the flight. It did not take long to get through customs and head to the waiting lounge. When I checked my watch again, it was fifteen minutes before boarding. I could not afford to waste time, so I went straight to the boarding gate. When I reached it, the place was nearly empty as all the passengers had just left. My heart was racing, thinking that I might have missed the flight. The boarding lounge staff greeted me with a smile when I showed them my boarding pass and my suit case before warning me to move quickly as the plane was about to take-off. As I walked into the plane, I saw many of the passengers were already seated. As I settled into my seat and checked my watch, it was 1.00pm. Soon I found out from the other passengers that the plane had been delayed by an hour. I realised then that I might not have made it if the flight had been on time. Once again, I thanked my dad for delaying the flight so that I could make it.

The smell of chicken curry soon interrupted my thoughts; I had only had a cup of coffee for breakfast. It did not take long before I finished my lunch with my fingers while some travellers were still struggling with a knife and fork. Soon after my lunch, I was waiting for the in-flight drinks. The influence of the Scottish culture for the last five years had improved my alcohol tolerance, especially for whisky. After the first one to quench my thirst, I had another four shots before I heard the announcement to fasten our seatbelts as the plane was about to land in Bangkok. It was around 2.00pm local time when I arrived at the Bangkok International Airport.

When I saw Bangkok, I thought that I had overcome all the hurdles following my wedding. From Bangkok onwards I hoped my journey would be smooth, but I did not realise there was another new episode waiting for me!

I remembered my agent had mentioned that my connecting flight on the same day was at 11.50pm from the Bangkok International Airport. I thought about what I could do until 11.00pm in Bangkok. I went to the reception at the airport and explained that I was in transit to London, but I had to wait until midnight, which was more than ten hours. The receptionist had a look at my ticket and said that under the International Air Traffic Association Agreement, I was entitled to a break with hotel accommodation and a meal paid for by the airline. Soon I received a meal voucher, a hotel room reservation slip and the necessary dockets for shuttle service from the airport to the hotel. I quickly got into the shuttle bus that was transporting the passengers and their belongings to the nominated hotel. The driver of the shuttle bus was a Thai local and his conversational English was excellent.

As soon as we reached the hotel, I had several porters attempting to help me carry my luggage to my room with the hope of a good tip. Although I tried several times to let them know that I was fit enough to carry my own luggage, I

< 9 > Unexpected hurdles after my wedding

realised that those men worked very hard to earn their living, so I allowed one to help me. The porter who helped me was very happy with my generous tip and stayed back to chat with me to find out if I needed any further help. He also left his private telephone number so I could call him if I nee]ded any further help before I left the hotel.

The hotel was an impressive building. As I walked through to my room it was comfortably cool. The rooms were large with a queen-size bed, a large bathroom with a shower and bath, and ample space to unload my luggage. There was a clean dressing-gown, a pair of slippers, an ironing board and a few drinks in the bar fridge. The bath was lined with additional items such as lotions, towels, facecloths, tissues, and bathmats. The clean bathroom was adjacent to the modern shower facility with bright lights and good ventilation. I was pleasantly surprised as I did not expect such a nice room as a guest on a complimentary stay. I had a nice, cold shower to refresh myself and then went to reception to remind the hotel staff about my transport to the airport. I was glad to note that the reception had already reserved a taxi to fetch me at 7.30pm from the hotel. They reminded me to be on time as it took more than an hour to reach the airport. I knew that I could not afford to make any mistakes, so I wandered down to the shops at the nearby emporium instead of going into Bangkok. I enjoyed seeing Thai handicrafts as I walked around the emporium. Time flew by and it was getting closer to 6.00pm when I looked at my watch and decided to have my evening meal before getting my pre-booked taxi.

I soon discovered that the meal voucher had a maximum

value of THB120, which was only enough to have a bowl of tom yum (a sour soup made with prawn paste), but not enough for a main meal. I was happy to pay the extra cost to fill my stomach for the evening. As the restaurant was comfortably air conditioned, my appetite increased and I ordered several more dishes, as this was a one-time opportunity to eat authentic Thai food. With a heavy stomach, I returned to my room to tidy myself up before I had my luggage taken to reception. By 6.45pm I was at the reception area with my luggage and not long after the reserved taxi arrived. The driver helped me to transfer my single piece luggage into the taxi. Before leaving the hotel, I thanked the receptionist for the room and the warm hospitality given to me for the past few hours. Again, I tipped the porter for his help and got into the back seat of the taxi, as the driver suggested. At that moment I felt everything was going to be fine, but I did not know what was about to happen!

The driver looked about forty-five years old, a local person who spoke very little English. We could not communicate because I knew no Thai. I introduced myself in English, but I'm not sure he understood what I said. He nodded his head with a smile and quickly turned away to drive the car. Only minutes into our journey, we were on the highway when it began to rain, quickly turning into a thunderstorm.

As I was seated in the rear of the car, I did not realise how heavily it had been raining until I looked through the rear window and noticed that the road was flooded with at least six inches of water. The rain was coming down as if someone was pouring buckets of water, non-stop. I was not too worried

< 9 > Unexpected hurdles after my wedding

because I felt safe in the car, but that feeling soon disappeared when I realised my shoes were a bit wet. I became worried and looked carefully at the floor, amazed to notice about two inches of water down there. I panicked and, pointing to my feet, started yelling, 'Water, water, here, here!' The driver did not seem surprised, so I assumed he understood what I trying to say and perhaps he knew that the car was not completely waterproof.

He quickly stopped the car and gestured, inviting me to come into the front seat. As he started driving again, the storm got stronger. I could hardly see the road and wondered how he was still managing to drive. I could only see the pouring rain on the car window, its direction constantly changing with the strong wind. I saw that either side of the road had pools of water which had been rice fields before the rain but now they were completely underwater.

As he drove, the water level on the road was rising and I noticed that water was also coming through the floor in the front of the car. There was frequent lightning followed by thunder ahead of us. Slowly, the sky was turning dark and I was beginning to panic. I hoped and prayed that the road to the airport was not blocked because of the floods.

Before I finished my prayer, the car jerked and slowed down and after a few minutes it finally stopped. I panicked further and looked at the driver anxiously. The driver seemed frightened and quickly got out to check something under the bonnet before returning to start the car. There was a noise when he turned the key, but the engine would not start. I was no help to him because I had no idea how to do even basic mechanical repairs. I definitely knew that the engine would not start. Meanwhile, the car was in the middle of the road so the driver had to quickly push it to the side. I could not sit still and watch the driver push the car by himself, so I helped him move his car quickly, even though I knew I would get soaked in the rain. We could not communicate with each other, but he knew that I was not pleased with his service. I was angry, frustrated and totally helpless.

I looked at my watch and panicked more as it showed 7.30pm. I knew that I had to be at the airport around 8.00pm to confirm my seat for the connecting flight to London. I felt frustrated in the situation as I had not expected this. I expected that the hotel would have a backup strategy in emergency situations like this.

I took my luggage out of the car and placed it on the bus stop bench on the roadside. The small, tin roof top was hardly enough to cover me from the thunderstorm. The driver looked at me helplessly; he was saying something in Thai, which was useless, because even if I understood him, I was too angry to listen.

A sudden chill ran down my spine; I felt very lonely standing on the roadside in the pouring rain in a strange country looking for a vehicle to hitch a lift with. There were no vehicles in sight; I assumed the local people were fully aware of the thunderstorm and had probably avoided travelling in such bad weather. It was quite unusual to not find any vehicles on the main road to an international airport.

When I looked at my watch and noted it was 8.00pm, I became more panicky and did not know how I was going to

< 9 > Unexpected hurdles after my wedding

be rescued. Once again I looked up in the sky and called for my father. 'Dad, where are you? You know that I need your help. I have only called on you when I am desperate'. If anyone had seen me at that moment, they would have thought I was a lunatic standing near a main road looking up at the sky in the pouring rain, yelling.

I did not know what else to do, or how to get to the airport on time. I had been warned that if I missed the flight, I had no chance of joining my wife's flight to London. After calling for help, I began to see some cars on the road going towards the airport. I waved at every vehicle to stop and rescue me. I wondered whether the drivers were able to see me as the visibility was so bad. I had no idea how far I was from the airport, but I assumed it must be in the same direction we had been travelling. I kept waving to any oncoming vehicles, with no luck.

I was losing hope as time was ticking away and my luck seemed to have gone. The situation was looking incredibly hopeless. I continued to pray harder, yelling out for my dad's help. Within a few minutes, I saw a panel van coming. I quickly took out my handkerchief and waved at the van. To my amazement, the van slowed down and finally stopped. I was not sure how I was going to explain to the driver that I needed a lift to the airport. Strangely, without exchanging a single word, he pointed to the seat next to him and smiled for me to get in.

I quickly grabbed my suitcase and placed in the back of the van as there was only just enough room for me in the front seat next to the driver. The rain was still pouring with no sign of slowing down. I knew that my suitcase would be wet in the back of the panel van, but I had no choice. As soon as I was in the van, he started moving.

From my pick-up point to the airport, there was no conversation between the driver and me. My situation that day was so desperate that I didn't notice it at the time, but it was quite unusual for a local driver to not make any attempt to talk to me as he was rescuing me. Not long after, the airport became visible and my heart slowed down as we approached it. Before we reached the terminal, he decided to drop me a few metres away from the unloading sign. As I was retrieving my luggage, he drove away without waiting for me to thank him, say goodbye, or even to receive a tip.

As soon as I got my luggage, I quickly rushed to stand in the long queue at the airport check-in counter. While I was standing in the queue and calming down, I thought about the trip I had just managed from the hotel to the airport. I began to think about the stranger who had rescued me from my desperate circumstance. There were few things that puzzled me.

Firstly, I could not remember the driver as I did not even really see him. He did not say a word throughout the journey. The second thought was that the stranger knew where to take me without asking. The third mystery was that my luggage was dry when I picked it up from the back of the van. I could not believe my luggage was dry when it had been in the pouring rain. The final strange fact was that the driver did not wait for a tip for his help. Without his help, I don't know what could have happened to me. I could not have been at the

< 9 >   Unexpected hurdles after my wedding

airport on time to be on the same flight as Suba. I wondered what Suba would have done if I had not been there.

My conclusion was that it must have been my dad's help. He must have heard my pleas. Without his help on that day, things would not have happened. To this day, the whole experience seems like a dream.

Still in my dream world, I had forgotten that I had not yet started my return journey to the UK yet. Just before 10.00pm I heard the boarding call. As I walked into the plane, I was relieved to see Suba seated not far from my allocated seat.

After the usual checks for take-off, I heard the pilot's departure announcement. It was well after 1.00am when the plane finally left Bangkok. At that moment I felt very relaxed and knew I was heading towards my destination at last. As soon as the plane was airborne, I eagerly awaited my first scotch. Before too long, I had a double scotch with ice and reflected on my wedding trip.

I was glad the hassles of my wedding were behind me and was looking forward to starting my new role as a husband. If I had known about all the hurdles I was going to face, I would not have gone to Malaysia to get married. Suba and I had hoped the wedding would be simple and hassle-free, but we had ended up experiencing some unpleasant events.

I waited for the meal service to be over before I approached one of the air hostesses, asking if I could change my seat with the passenger seated next to Suba. The hostess spoke to the lady and got her permission to swap. I quickly shifted next to Suba.

It was quite a different experience to be seated together

officially as husband and wife. Before the wedding we were very relaxed and friendly, but after the wedding there was some kind of reservation. I wondered why Suba had not given me her total support when I was in need. Her overtly uncooperative behaviour during the wedding was still annoying me. My family thought that I was madly in love with her, while she showed no interest in me. Although my eyes were shut on the plane, my thoughts were going wild while I was sat next to Suba. Before long, my thoughts moved towards my brother, Krish. I was wondering how he would have reacted when he heard about the unpleasant incidents during my unapproved wedding.

The return journey seemed quicker than I expected. I heard the captain ask the crew to prepare for landing and for the passengers to have their travel documents handy. As I opened and looked at my passport just before the plane landed, I panicked because of my re-entry visa. My UK visa had been granted for three years so that I could study, but my nursing study was over I did not have a return-to-study visa. Technically, I had no grounds to return to Scotland. I was nervous, but did not have a choice because we were in the queue and just about to face the immigration officer.

Suba was the first one to be assessed. He looked at her passport and did not hesitate to stamp it. When I moved forward with my passport, he raised his eyebrows, until I showed him my letter of offer to study in Scotland. After several questions, the immigration officer queried my relationship with Suba. When we produced our marriage certificate, he smiled for a second and told me to sort out my

< 9 > Unexpected hurdles after my wedding

visa within the remaining three months I had for nursing. He quickly stamped my passport and wished us good luck. As soon as I took a few steps away, I opened my passport to check my visa status and was relieved to note that he had stamped a three-month visa.

I was glad the legitimate entry approval would allow me to stay in UK to pursue my education. I had a moment of internal joy because I had waited such a long time in my life to commence my degree.

We did not have to wait too long before we collected our luggage and headed to the taxi stand to join the queue. From the London train station, we transferred onto a Dundee-bound train, a journey that took eighteen hours. Luckily, the places we had booked had plenty of vacant seats to stretch out onto. Throughout the journey, we slept comfortably using the seats next to us. Suba appeared as relaxed as I was, and I was happy to leave the wedding hassles back in Malaysia.

We were tired but pleased to reach my apartment in Dundee. Although Suba had been to my place, I felt very uncomfortable bringing my new wife to such a place. I would have loved to take her to a well-furnished, three-bedroom apartment to start our new life, but my circumstances did not permit it. Fortunately, we both knew the terrible accommodation situation was only a short-term survival strategy.

‹ 10 ›

Getting what I wanted

On arriving at my apartment, we discussed our situation and how we had to manage it. We agreed to be thrifty as our finances were tight. We agreed to cook meals at home instead of eating out. As the rent was minimal, it did not affect our budget. Our primary concern was my undergraduate tuition fees.

As we were settling in, I made some enquiries about fee assistance as a full-time student at Aberdeen University. I found out from the registry that I was eligible to apply for a study grant. According to the study grant guidelines, I needed to have worked in the UK for three years and paid income tax prior to my full-time studies. I quickly submitted my application and waited for the reply. I also found out that there were several student residences available for married full time students with no children. After applying, I was interviewed and told that the accommodation would be available a week after classes had commenced.

We were glad that I would not have to travel to Aberdeen

from Dundee. We moved all our things to Aberdeen in a hired car. Suba was familiar with the city as she had completed her midwifery qualification at Aberdeen Royal Infirmary. The city was a novelty for me. I found it clean and spacious, a bit different to Dundee. The city attracted visitors from all over the world with its growing oil economy. The granite buildings were quite unique with beautifully maintained gardens along the roadside.

The university residence was in a row of professional suites, in which two large houses were allocated as university residences. The three-storey building had a common kitchen with a dining room next to it, as well as a basement. It also had one telephone for all of the residents to share. The rooms were partly furnished with double beds and mattresses, and also a table to study at. The carpets, bathrooms and toilets were cleaned regularly by university domestic staff.

Our allocated room was in the attic on the third floor, with a good view of the street from the only window in the room. Our room was smaller than most of the others, but it was big enough for us. I was happy with the university accommodation as that was the first time in my life that I had such a comfortable room for my studies. We had a table next to the window and a queen-size bed with a thick quilt for the cold Aberdeen weather. There was a bedside table with a lamp, a wardrobe and a bedside shelf for books, which made bedtime reading very convenient. There were shower and bath facilities on every storey, so there were no queues. The large pantry at the ground level was available for all residents to store their groceries and the four large refrigerators were large enough for all twelve couples to share. The fully equipped kitchen had several grills and ovens for the residents to prepare their meals at any time and to enjoy them in the adjoining dining room.

Suba and I were excited with the superior facilities. Suba was happy to have refrigerators available to store our milk and perishables, rather than hanging them outside in the cold as we had done in Whitfield. The residence was centrally heated all the time, unlike my Whitfield apartment which was nearly always cold. We enjoyed daily hot baths and showers and sometimes we had more than one shower to quickly warm ourselves up, especially in winter.

Despite our poor financial situation, we were both happy as we were together. For the week I was attending class before moving, I had been away from home for twelve hours each day travelling between Dundee and Aberdeen and attending class. It was a painful experience and we did not want to miss each other again for even a minute. At that time, we did not have sufficient cash for our daily expenses, but we were grateful that we had warm, comfortable, fully-furnished accommodation. We agreed that we should enjoy our time in Aberdeen as a newly-wedded couple as long as we could manage our expenses. As neither of us was working when I started university, the little savings we had were just enough to cover our food expenses, but not for long. Suba was keen to get back to work as soon as possible.

When the university semester started, I had the emotional challenge of leaving Suba at home while I was away at lectures. We both found it was difficult to wake up from the warm bed every morning for breakfast during the cold winters. I often

< 10 > Getting what I wanted

wore a pair of jeans and a thick pullover to keep me warm before leaving the apartment. The morning walk from the residence to university campus became my revision session as well; I held my small notecards as I walked the seventy-five minutes each morning; which also helped me to take my mind off Suba.

My first four semester subjects had practical classes that went from 3.00pm to 6.00pm. I often wrote my laboratory reports in class soon after my practicals and completed them within the allocated three hours before going home. When I was home, I spent the rest of the day with Suba.

On my way from university, I often bought groceries for our dinner that we prepared together after our shower. At that time, Suba did not know how to cook, so I prepared most of the meals. We often had white rice, green vegetables and chicken wings, or spare ribs and an occasional bottle of sparkling wine between us to finish our dinner. As soon as we finished our dinner, we tidied the kitchen.

We spent some quality quiet moments to ourselves before we came downstairs to the common room to watch the 7.00pm news. We usually stayed downstairs until 9.00pm, unless I had any unfinished study or wanted to play a game of Scrabble. On occasion, we went for walks in the park, despite the cold, howling wind. We seldom went to the movies because it cost us money which we did not have. During those days we were not bothered about the cash that we did not have as we were happy to be together.

Although we adjusted to our living situation easily, coping with university study and passing my examinations was an ongoing challenge for me.

When I started my undergraduate course, I was twenty-seven years old, whereas many of my classmates were in their early twenties. Most of them were unmarried and resided in university halls of residence, which were more expensive, but closer to the lecture theatres. I lost three hours a day on travel instead of doing university work. Those who lived in the halls of residence had a great social network with readily available peer support. Learning science at university level without high school preparation was stressful for me, whereas my peers had studied science through their school years.

During my undergraduate study, there were several students in my class who were from overseas. During my first year, I was fortunate to know an international student named Khaled, who was smart and supportive. After class we compared our lecture notes and revised our work in the nearest library. The next day we compared our homework answers. Khaled would usually have nearly finished answering all the questions while I would still be struggling with the first few.

Another supportive chemistry tutorial partner was Shalini. Her advanced knowledge in chemistry assisted us in completing the experiments and reports before leaving the laboratory. I regularly answered past examination questions to be checked by my lecturers, slowly gaining my confidence and subsequently reducing my anxiety as the final examinations approached.

As time progressed, our financial position was getting worse and we had not heard the outcome of my grant application. I had enquired several times through the Student

Union Office, as advised by the Registry Office, with no options except to wait. When we were almost out of cash for food, Suba decided to go to work.

It did not take long before she was employed full-time in a hospital that was about fifteen minutes by bus. As Suba had completed her registrations in midwifery and general nursing, she was well qualified for the position as a Division 1 Registered Nurse. I adjusted my study times to suit her shifts. When Suba was up at 6am for her morning shift, we had our breakfast together before I escorted her to catch the bus to work. I did most of my study before she returned from work and made sure dinner was prepared. When Suba started working, our financial position improved, but we still continued to take our home-cooked lunches rather than buying them.

On weekends, when she had no shifts, we travelled outside Aberdeen or visited our friends in Dundee. On other days we went for long walks, enjoying the beautiful parks and gardens of Aberdeen. The clean beaches were an attraction, but the water was not warm enough to swim in, even in the summer.

After several months of stressful waiting, we received a note from the Scottish Education Department stating I was successful in my study grant application. We were both excited to receive the long-awaited good news because it covered our accommodation debts while Suba's income was sufficient enough to feed us and purchase the necessary items for our daily living.

Not long after, we decided to purchase a second-hand Austin Morris to reduce my walking time to university. It also assisted with our weekly shopping load that we had struggled to carry from the supermarkets. More importantly, it meant Suba avoided the long wait to catch the bus on the cold winter mornings. We also used it to visit our friends on weekends when Suba was not working.

I had several jobs during my semester breaks to earn some cash. There was one memorable work experience as a porter in Aberdeen City Hospital that I will never forget.

The hospital was old with wards separated by tar roads. Sometimes visitors parked their vehicles next to the wards under the nearby trees for easy access. I worked twelve-hour shifts as a porter during my semester break. The work was very physically strenuous, with certain tasks to be completed within a short time. As a young recruit, my 6.00am task was to deliver milk to the wards in crates using a battery-operated van. Loading and unloading the milk crates in the morning was initially embarrassing as the sixty-five-year-old porters were carrying two crates of milk bottles at a time while I struggled to lift one crate.

The next task was the lunch delivery to the wards around midday using a trailer. Trolleys, each with several trays of hot lunches, were pushed onto the back of the trailer using a ramp that was pulled by a van. All the trolleys loaded in the back of the van had to be tightly secured before driving the van on the uneven road in the hospital compound. In the hilly areas, the van lost its speed and sometimes slipped back in reverse. I soon learned to speed up around the hilly areas after a few failed attempts where I nearly lost the lunch trolley.

Another unforgettable task was specimen collection. The usual task on a night shift was to collect specimens from the

< 10 > Getting what I wanted

wards that needed to be stored in a centralised refrigerator in the 'spooky' Virology Department. Although the task was easy, finding the refrigerator on a quiet, windy night, with only a torch, in the completely dark big building, was frightening. As soon as I placed the specimens in the fridge, I raced out of the building right away.

The spookiest things I had to do on nights was to collect the bodies of deceased patients from the wards to store them in the mortuary freezer. My subconscious mind recalled stories I had heard as a child; frightening stories of how dead people suddenly woke up, so when I had to open the mortuary to get the trolley, I was petrified. One of the trolley wheels would make quite a loud noise on my way to pick up the body, but was quiet on my return with the body to the mortuary. In the ward, I had help from the staff transfer the body from the hospital bed to the trolley, but when loading the body from the trolley onto the mortuary shelves, I was on my own.

I had to push the loaded trolley from the ward to the mortuary, which meant walking in the icy cold weather against strong winds that tried to push me off the road. Sometimes, I had to wait for the winds to slow down before I continued. On some miserable nights it could take me thirty minutes of fighting to reach the mortuary. I would have to unlock the door, turn on the lights and push the trolley inside by myself. By then, I was shivering with fright and the cold. To make matters worse, I had to document any visible scars or jewellery on the patient's body. After recording the required details, I had to transfer the body from the trolley to one of the freezer shelves. The empty freezer shelf had to be carefully lined up next to the trolley so that the body could be dragged onto the shelf without lifting. Prior to moving the body, the brakes had to be on to stop the trolley moving.

The draw sheet under the body was enough to drag it onto the shelf. The drag started with the top end, then the tail end and finally the middle, even though the person had died, the body still had to be treated with great care and respect. On my first few attempts, I nearly dropped the body on the floor. As soon as I finished, I instantly left the mortuary. I often prayed not be called to fetch another body on the same night. I will never forget those experiences.

Despite its challenging moments, vacation work did contribute some cash towards home expenses. Not long before completing my first year of study successfully, we moved to private accommodation, which was cheaper and closer to several shops and other amenities, although it was far noisier. The limited parallel parking spots between the maple trees along the road froze in winter. The two feet of snow between the trees had to be cleared before moving the cars. The apartment also had a small garden at the back where I attempted several times to grow vegetables, but only ended up with uninvited slugs.

The place we rented was semi-furnished with antique furniture that only Suba liked. The old, low-capacity washing machine was noisy one and moved around when in use, and the only bed was a single, which was a bit of a tight squeeze for both of us. The small kitchenette did not entice us to use the kitchen much. We did not store too much food in the small refrigerator or pantry, but luckily the shops were close. The hot water service only supplied five minutes of hot water with a ten-minute wait before it heated up again. The thick carpet was not easy to vacuum. The only heat was a wall gas heater in the lounge that didn't heat the bedrooms. The gaps in those old windows could not stop the cold breeze from coming in. Despite all these limitations, it offered us a lot more privacy, which was important to us.

I continued my undergraduate course, while Suba was busy with her full-time work, until she heard about Health Visiting (HV). Through her friends she found out about HV course offered by the Robert Gordon Institute of Technology (RGIT) in Aberdeen. We agreed that the course would be a useful qualification to further Suba's career. We also thought it would be great if both of us were studying at the same time so that we could do more things together. Suba's work experience with the Grampians Health Board (GHB) meant that she definitely met the entry requirement, but she still had to be sponsored by the GHB. Unfortunately, as the sponsorship quota was already full for the year, she was unsuccessful, but the GHB enclosed a note encouraging her to re-apply in time for the next intake.

Suba was too disappointed to re-apply. Six weeks later, I tried to convince her, but she found it very difficult to even to fill in the application form. I ended up filling in the form for her, as she was convinced it was a waste of time. Despite her ongoing reluctance, I spent a week on her application before getting her signature and submitting it again. By this time, Suba had completely lost interest in the course and only signed the form to please me.

Four weeks later, she had a letter waiting for her to read

after work. An amazed smile appeared on her face as she read it. She could not believe she had been offered a place in the course. We were excited and spoke about what this would involve for us, and Suba was enthusiastic and spoke to her friends who had completed the course. The following day she went to RGIT to accept the offer in writing and collect all the necessary documents and her booklist to plan her studies.

Not long after the offer, Suba commenced her study and our daily routine changed again. We were very fortunate we got home around the same time and had lecture-free weekends together. As Suba had to go in the opposite direction to her campus in the mornings, I often dropped her off before going to my classes. By 5.00pm we were both home and at 7.00pm we went to the library to study after a quick dinner. We found that our practice of studying regularly in the evenings kept us on par with the high achievers in our classes.

Most weekends, we left for the library at 9.00am and came home about 1pm to prepare our lunch. At 2.00pm we went shopping for the week. In the evenings we relaxed we visited our friends or went for leisurely walks in the beautiful parks and gardens of Aberdeen. Some weekends we were up early and keen to complete a 10km walk before 10am to maintain our fitness. We had a busy study life and barely noticed the twelve months that passed us by.

Not long after her graduation, Suba was offered a position as a health visitor with the Grampians Region. She was excited to reap the results of her hard work. Health Visitor Suba was attached to a multi-disciplinary team in a group practice. She enjoyed cycling to work and to her clients' appointments.

Most evenings, she was home and we cooked our dinners. Suba's income allowed us to enjoy occasional cinema visits, trips to the countryside and more importantly, visiting our Malaysian friends, who lived outside Aberdeen.

During this year, one day I had a call from Gana to inform us that he was going to marry Angie, although he was not sure it was the right move. Although I was married, I was not a marriage counsellor, so I could only advise Gana that no marriage was guaranteed to be successful. Hindus who believed that arranged marriages last a lifetime had been disappointed as they often ended in failure. Obviously, Angie's family preferred she marry someone Chinese, while Gana's side would have liked an Indian bride for him. I knew their commitment to live together would have ongoing challenges.

I agreed to be in Dundee a few days before the wedding so that I could organise the reception and catering for the fifty guests of Scottish, English, Irish, Welsh, Mauritian, Malaysian, Chinese and Indian backgrounds. As soon as I reached Gana's residence on Friday afternoon after my lectures, I organised a team of experienced cooking volunteers to help me prepare a wedding lunch with a strong Asian flavour. I cooked the Malaysian-Indian- style meat dishes and Yap (Angie's good friend) prepared several authentic Chinese dishes.

Gana also wanted me to be his best man, which I happily agreed to without understanding the commitments of the role. On the day of the wedding, Gana was driven to the registration office by his friend, while I drove Angie. Unfortunately, I left my suit in Aberdeen and I didn't have time to drive back, so I had to search for Gana's largest suit, as he was much slimmer than me. This meant I was late in bringing Angie to the registration office, but fortunately, it was quite acceptable for the bride to arrive late. Following their solemn oaths and signatures, the newly-wedded couple and their guests proceeded to Gana's residence for the lunch reception. As the reception chief, I made sure that food and drinks were served continuously for the guests as soon as they walked in with their gifts. Later that evening, the wedding celebration moved to the nearest pub, the Kettle Drum.

There were approximately thirty new guests at the pub before the wedding cake was cut. As the best man, I had my very first public speaking experience and I received a few congratulatory remarks. The six large bottles of scotch certainly helped the party to be one of the most enjoyable we'd had. A few other guests came as the evening progressed. Unfortunately, the pub closed at midnight, but as the guests were in full party mode, the whole crowd continued the party at Gana's residence, only a five-minute walk away. The drinks and nibbles continued until around 2.00am, when the crowd slowly began to thin out. Amazingly, Angie and Gana were still awake, but totally exhausted by the time all the guests had left. Suba and I left Dundee the next day to be home by Sunday evening, as I had lectures on Monday morning.

One of the best things during my third year of study was the opportunity to revise my university lectures during my semester vacation job as a security guard.

When I was on my twelve-hour shift, I always had my university notes with me so that I could look at them during my free moments. By the first hour into the shift, all the initial and essential checks had to be done and then the supervision of premises had to be continued at regular intervals until the shift finished. In between the regular checks, I managed to find time to revise my university lectures.

The Securicor Company that employed me had several premises in Aberdeen that were also very conducive to study. I found the ergonomic tables and chairs had good lighting and suited me far better than my desk at home.

The site managers were very supportive and often asked me to help myself with the office items, such as notepads and pens and so on, which saved me money. I was also lucky that the friendly and supportive staff at the company made my vacation work relaxed and enjoyable. When I returned to university lectures, I not only had some cash, but had also revised my lectures. Capitalising on those vacation opportunities enabled me to achieve results good enough to be invited into my fourth year of the Undergraduate Honours program.

I was excited to receive a special letter from the Professor of the Department of Zoology inviting me to commence my fourth year Honours study in Zoology. I was thrilled to receive the invitation because some of the students who wanted to enrol in Honours study, who were much younger than me, were denied, based on their examination results. At that moment, I gave myself a pat on the back, finally feeling equal to my younger classmates.

The fourth year study was very intense for the twenty-eight specially selected students in my Honours year. All those special recruits were given keys to the building with full access at any time. The individual cubicles for Honours students were a great benefit because they allowed us to continue our experiments without interruption. My research on house crickets (*Acheta domesticus*), examined the effects of anti-juvenile hormones on their development and metabolism. Although the allocated duration time for fourth year research was six months fulltime, the majority of us did the equivalent of twelve months fulltime research. Like many of my peers, I was often researching on the weekends as well.

Just about the time I commenced my fourth year, Suba had changed her job from Health Visitor to a Charge Nurse position at Aberdeen Royal Infirmary (ARI). I supported her decision as there were more opportunities for her career progression at the hospital. Certainly, her education and experience in nursing, midwifery and health visiting had prepared her well for a senior clinical position. Furthermore, ARI was closer to the house and it would take her 15 minutes to walk there.

Again, Suba and I had to re-organise our daily routine. Usually, I dropped Suba off at work, then continued my research at the Department of Zoology. There were odd days when I had to continue my experiments non-stop for forty-eight hours, and sometimes the supportive academic staff and PhD students in the department dropped in for a friendly chat to find out if we had any questions about our experiments.

One of the main reasons for my honours study was to pursue medicine. Unfortunately, after I began my fourth year, there were changes to the Scottish Education Department grants. The Scottish Government decided to fund students for only one undergraduate study, so if I wanted to study medicine, I would only be given a grant for a further two years because I had already been funded for four years. At that time, I was in no position to support myself for full-time study.

Suba and I were very disappointed about the changes and how they impacted my career path. Despite the disappointment, we were absolutely appreciative of the support given to me to do my undergraduate degree. So, instead of thinking about medicine, I decided that I would explore doing a postgraduate course that could be completed quickly and allow me to earn a decent income.

After searching for several months, I found that the most popular courses at that time were Chartered Accountancy (CA) and the Master of Business Administration (MBA). I had no knowledge about those courses, but I knew the employment market for them was good and that my Honours degree would qualify me for admission. After reading several university brochures and personal discussions with professionals in those fields, I decided to pursue MBA.

My admission to MBA at Edinburgh University for the twelve-month course was conditional on a first or second class Honours degree and successful clearance of the Graduate Management Admission Test (GMAT). I had heard that the GMAT was a difficult test to pass, so I familiarised myself with questions directly from Princeton while still completing my Honours year. Not long after I submitted my application for the MBA program, I was delighted to receive an offer of a place only with my Honours requirement, meaning I didn't have to sit the GMAT. When I shared the great news with Suba, she was thrilled to know there was an alternative career to medicine.

‹ 11 ›

The career plan that went wrong

With my study plan to pursue with an MBA at Edinburgh decided, we began seriously thinking about starting our own family. Suba and I had been married for more than three years before we talked about having children. We were aware that as we aged the probability of having a healthy baby would be impacted. We had worked in hospitals and cared for children with birth defects, some of which were the result of having children when older. We carefully calculated that our first child should be born soon after my fourth year examinations and not before. We chose the name Anand for a boy or Anuja if the child was a girl.

Suba fell pregnant and, with her due date in August, she continued working full-time at the hospital. When I finished my fourth year examinations in May 1981, I started work immediately as a Registered Nurse in the Forensic Unit at the Aberdeen Royal Cornhill Hospital (RCH). My workmates were cognizant of my limited psychiatric experience, but always encouraged me to ask them for help. The work culture

< 11 >   The career plan that went wrong

at the RCH was inclusive, supportive and sociable, which made my job enjoyable, and Suba was also enjoying her work at the Aberdeen Royal Infirmary as a Charge Nurse.

We were keen to be parents for the first time and enjoyed quality moments together. We took many walks to the beautiful parks across the road from where we lived and had spent many hours on the swings, seesaws and slides, reliving our childhood days. Most of the time we talked about our unborn child and our future. On many evenings we ended up at Gana and Angie's place, which was only a kilometre away. Suba often enjoyed the walk to their place through the hospital grounds under the shade of the majestic oak trees. As we walked, we admired the beautiful flowers, the busy bees at work and birds that dropped in for a drink at their garden fountains. Suba found the walks helped her to relax and sleep better at night.

Gana and Angie were usually home from work by 5.00pm. They often looked forward to our visits, and we often ended up staying at their place for dinner, our conversations going well into the night. Sometimes when Gana drove us home, it was after midnight.

In June 1981, I achieved my Second Class Honours degree. Suba and I were very happy that I had fulfilled the conditional offer for entry into the MBA program. I was confident that my grant would support my MBA in October that year. Meanwhile, I enjoyed my work and prepared for my graduation in July that year.

The strict graduation details specified that I wear a dark or grey suit with a black tie and white shirt. We knew that purchasing the graduation attire would be expensive, but we had no other choice. As the graduation ceremony was approaching, Suba's body shape was changing and her old clothes were no longer fitting well, but she was equally keen to attend my graduation ceremony.

On the graduation day, Suba's big belly contour was quite noticeable through her very loose dress. Obviously, the local media was not able to bypass her without a chat. We were interviewed for a few minutes about our cultural background and the names we had chosen for the baby.

Soon after the interview all graduands were invited into the fully-occupied hall that held one thousand guests. Suba was invited to sit in the front row just across from the Vice Chancellor, who delivered the speech. She was very excited to see me on the stage to receive my testamur because it was our collaborative hard work that enabled me to complete the course successfully. Gana and Angie, my special family, were also there and proud of my achievement.

To me, that day was a great moment of joy after the hard work in our lives. I always wanted to be a graduate and poverty had held me back, but I had finally made it! I thanked my father in Heaven who had guided me during my difficult times. The day was also sad as my mother was not there to share my great achievement, even though she would not have understood the value of my qualification. That day finished with a sumptuous meal prepared by Angie and Gana, followed by a few drinks of Scotch.

The next day, we were on the local news. My mates at work, who had read the local news, congratulated me for my achievements and understood about me from the local paper.

< 11 > The career plan that went wrong

After my graduation, I continued working in the forensic unit, while Suba began her maternity leave in July, about four weeks prior to her due date. One night, she became restless and woke me from my deep sleep after calling the hospital to be admitted. She was anxious to go to the maternity unit because her water had broken. I quickly helped her to the warmed-up car in the cold morning. I held her close to me as we slowly walked down the two flights of stairs to the car with her hospital luggage.

We arrived at the hospital around 1.00am. The hospital was quiet as we walked through as most of the patients were asleep, but as soon we reached the maternity wing, it became noisier. The nurses received us very warmly when we registered at the station, and I took a seat while Suba had a wash before she changed into the hospital gown to be examined by the obstetrician.

We did not know what to expect as soon as Suba was settled in bed, but we prayed that our baby would be born healthy. While Suba was lying in bed, she became uncomfortable because her contractions were intensifying and I was worried she might go into labour without the expert supervision of a midwife. Soon after, I conveyed her message to the nurse who was in charge, Suba's assigned midwife came to check her progress. I saw Suba's relief as soon as her midwife walked into her ward because she happened to be Suba's lecturer at RGIT.

About an hour later Suba's midwife was called away, but fortunately Suba was feeling calmer. As soon as Suba was relaxed, her contractions returned, stronger with increasing frequency. She felt a bit apprehensive because she did not see any midwives around her cubicle, but I assured her I could deliver the baby if necessary. An hour later her contractions began subsiding and she became very tired. As her energy was slipping, she was put on an intravenous dextrose infusion. As the day was breaking, I saw nurses and midwives arriving for their 7.30am duties. Suba's old lecturer dropped in to say goodbye as she was finishing her shift, but promised to be back later for her night shift.

The midwife in charge had noticed that I had not left Suba's side and that I looked exhausted. At about 8.00pm, she suggested that I should go home to freshen up and return. Suba nodded for me to go. I was very reluctant to leave at first, but as the apartment was only five minutes away and I had Suba's approval, I went home.

On my way home I dropped in to update Angie about Suba's situation. She was very surprised to hear that the baby had not been born yet. Angie saw my exhaustion and insisted that I change my clothes after a quick shower and have dinner at her place. By the time I had my shower, she had cooked dinner. After eating, I decided to sit for a couple of minutes to watch the news. I must have fallen asleep for two hours because when I woke up it was suddenly 10.30pm. I panicked because I had missed being next to Suba during her critical moments, and I rushed out of Angie's house, reaching the ward within ten minutes.

As I walked closer to Suba, I noticed she had an oxygen mask and felt that something had gone wrong. Her bed was tilted and not only was her blood pressure being monitored, but our unborn baby's heart rate and oxygen levels were also

< 11 > The career plan that went wrong

being monitored via an electrode on the foetus fontanelle. I was panicking, but kept myself calm. Suba was semiconscious with her eyes open but unable to talk. I made a note of all the health professionals looking after Suba, so that if things went wrong, I would know who to hold accountable.

I was still anxious about all the gadgets connected to her. I felt guilty that I had taken more than an hour to return after my wash and dinner. I began to recall the widespread news in the media at that time about hospital negligence in labour suites during deliveries. I was aware that the staff who were attending Suba were qualified and experienced, but I still wanted a guarantee that Suba and our baby were fine. At that moment, the only thing I could do was hold Suba's hand to reassure her. She could hardly keep her eyes open, but I kept on speaking to her. After the midwife's examination, the nurses noticed meconium staining, which meant the infant was in distress. The paediatrician was immediately called to confirm and decided to deliver the baby immediately.

I was sitting next to Suba and watched the busy, anxious staff around her with forceps to assist her delivery. The doctor rotated and shifted the baby's head with forceps to deliver the baby more easily and safely. It was a great relief when the baby was finally delivered after twenty-four hours of labour. Anand (our son) was examined for any obvious abnormalities by the paediatrician, who was concerned with his low birth weight. He recommended that Anand needed special nursery care for the next few days until his jaundice subsided and to prevent any further complications.

I spent time in the hospital with Suba while Anand was kept in the nursery most of the time, except for breastfeeding or when I was holding him in my arms. I took Suba's clothes home to be washed, and for the next few days I had delicious home-cooked meals at Gana's house, which I brought for Suba when I visited.

The news of our parenthood spread to our friends, who visited with presents. We wrote to our relatives in Malaysia about our child and the delivery experience, but most of the time our joy was shared with Gana and Angie.

After a week, Suba was discharged from hospital with Anand and we were not quite certain how to manage him at home. We got the necessary basics, such as a baby basinet to carry him in and out of the car, and a pram to push him around in. The pram was also to be his bed because we only had a single bed that Suba and I shared. We had some disposable nappies, but usually used cotton ones. Luckily, Suba managed to breastfeed Anand on demand after some early suckling struggles. After Anand had arrived, I was the one working full-time while Suba was caring for him at home. I often left for work in the morning and came home for lunch for some quick quality time with our newborn son, and sometimes some shopping. Whenever I was home, I attended to the bucket full of soiled nappies that kept on piling up.

With Anand's presence, the apartment was warm all the time, which was wonderful and also helped to dry our clothes indoors. We both enjoyed bathing Anand daily before we took him for a short walk in the park across from our apartment. Suba encouraged me to go out to join my workmates for a

< 11 >   The career plan that went wrong

break. I enjoyed drinks as a new father with my friends as they were the closest we had to a family in Scotland.

We started taking Anand for a stroll in his pram regularly, walking about four times a week and often ending up at Gana and Angie's, who would wait for us for dinner. Even though we did not have our parents or close families to support us, Angie and Gana's unconditional support was always there, and we were very grateful to have them.

Suba and I had several serious discussions about our future career paths when I completed my MBA. We were thinking about a country we could migrate to and safely bring up our children up. We discussed several places such as Brunei, a country in the island of Borneo where the main language was English. The second place was Canada, as several Malaysians had settled there after their studies. Australia was another destination where many Malaysians had already settled successfully. At the time of our discussions, Suba's older brother had already started his PhD in Civil Engineering at Queensland University in Australia and was living in Brisbane. According to him, the place was safe, with ideal weather. There were employment opportunities for graduates and the affordable houses were increasingly owned by new migrants. Our regular weekly calls to Brisbane encouraged our interest and led us to think that we should move there next.

While we were enjoying our new parenthood, I was excited to receive a letter confirming an MBA place at Edinburgh University. The offer was for an initial six-month Graduate Diploma in Business Administration, then to continue for another six months to complete the Master of Business

Administration. I made arrangements to live at the Edinburgh University married student accommodation during my course. Unfortunately, that accommodation was in old buildings with poor heating and substandard bathroom facilities that were not ideal for our newborn. We decided I would remain in Scotland to complete the MBA, while Suba and Anand would settle themselves in Australia with guidance from Faisal, who was studying at Queensland University.

Meanwhile, we applied and were interviewed by the Australian Embassy to migrate to Australia upon the completion of my MBA. While our migration plan was underway, we received a note to say that my Scottish Education Grant support application was not successful. Suba and I were very surprised because I met the entry criteria to the course, including three years full-time work experience and having contributed to UK superannuation. We could not do anything because there were strikes at that time and the Scottish Education Department (SED) was unreachable by telephone. As my accommodation and tuition costs would be unmanageable without the SED sponsorship, I had to call the university to cancel my reservations and to forego my MBA studies. Suba and I took a while to overcome our disappointment and revised our plan to move to Australia at the same time. Our financial position was very tight because I had only worked four months full-time during Suba's maternity leave and had not saved much, but we had just enough for our flights.

We planned to fly to Australia via Kuala Lumpur so that we could drop in to see our relatives. Our flight to Brisbane would

< 11 >   The career plan that went wrong

be in November that year, after I had resigned from my full-time position at the RCH. Within two weeks, our visas were approved with permanent resident status from the Australian Embassy. While we were packing for the journey, I received another letter from the SED approving my education grant to study my MBA at Edinburgh University. Unfortunately, that note arrived two weeks late as we had already decided to migrate to Australia.

We informed our landlady, Suba's friend, of our departure. We tidied the apartment as we packed our things. We did not have many possessions except for a Kenwood mixer, electric iron and Anand's clothes, all of which were carefully packed into two tea chests. Suba packed a few books, while we donated the rest to the library. The packed tea chests were sent through a sea carrier to be stored in Brisbane before we left Aberdeen. My friends were happy to accept the leftover alcohol, food, spices and other non-perishables as we cleaned the apartment.

I had arranged for Gana and my long-time classmate, Ken Shaw, who had taken time off from work, to be at the apartment around 7.00am on the day of our departure. They carried our heavy 32kg suitcases to the car down the two narrow flights of stairs. On that day, Ken had specially travelled to Aberdeen (about 100kms) to farewell me despite the very bad weather.

Heavy snowfalls in Scotland that day meant roads and air transport services were cancelled. We were lucky that none of our flights were cancelled on that day as it would have added further strain on us and our three-month-old baby.

Normally the journey could have taken thirty minutes, but, with the weather, it took Gana ninety minutes instead. We saw a few cars abandoned on the roadside in thirty centimetres of snow. Luckily, we reached Aberdeen Airport about an hour before the flight and had time to talk to Ken, who was expecting a private moment with us. After snapping a few photos at the airport, the final goodbyes were emotional, but Gana and Ken were glad for us to go and explore the greener pastures of our future. The remaining time was spent on the attention-seeking baby, who was fully wrapped in warm clothes and not sure what was happening to him.

After we had checked-in our luggage, we were happy to board the two-hour flight from Aberdeen to London with just our hand luggage. Once at Heathrow Airport, we found our way to the international terminal, carrying Anand and our hand luggage on our long and tiring walk. Inside the airport was comfortably warm, while snow continued falling outside the airport terminal.

We were tired when we boarded the plane around 7.00pm that day after attending to Anand's feeds and nappy changes.

As we had a three-month-old baby with us, we were called in before the other passengers to take a seat next to the movie screen in the economy section. The air hostess had hoisted the basinet for Anand by the time all the other international passengers were guided in. Although I'd had a good lunch at the Heathrow terminal, I was already looking forward to the in-flight dinner.

Before the plane started moving, Suba began breastfeeding Anand to prevent ear aches from cabin pressure changes. The

‹ 11 › The career plan that went wrong

atmosphere inside the plane turned busy as soon as the "fasten your seat belt" sign was turned off. Several of the passengers were waiting for their turn to use the restrooms, while others were busy reading the papers and magazines. Once the plane was fully airborne, a few of them started their walks along the aisles of the plane to stretch themselves.

About an hour later, Suba ordered a non-alcoholic drink, while I had a double Scotch with ginger ale. As Anand was settled in the basinet, both of us had a few quiet moments to finish our meals uninterrupted. The delicious food was a bit too much for Suba to finish without my help! While I was sipping my post-meal Scotch, Suba was already asleep, exhausted by travel and the baby. Both of us must have had an hour's sleep before we were woken up by Anand's cry. The light from the movie screen was sufficient for Suba to change his nappy.

After three hours of sitting, I took a stroll and found that there was a drinking party at the rear section of the plane. I joined the party for a few rounds of Scotch and got to know some passengers who were also migrating to Australia for a new start. When I opened my eyes in my seat, I realised there were only another seven hours left before we reached KL International Airport.

Most of our relatives had expected us to return to settle in Malaysia after our studies, but Suba and I had decided to stay away separately by ourselves for a while. We felt we had worked hard to complete our tertiary studies and wanted our marriage to be undisturbed by the caste differences between our families. Suba and I had talked about Australia and decided to test the ground for our future. If for some reason we did not like it there, we were prepared to move elsewhere or even to return to Malaysia.

We landed at KL International Airport around 10.00am on 13 November 1981. Suba and I felt the heat and humidity as we came out of the plane. When we left Aberdeen, I had my suit on to keep myself warm from the Aberdeen's wintry weather, but in KL I felt the heat even after removing my jacket in the air-conditioned airport terminal. Anand became restless as we carried him out of the plane.

We sighted my cousin, an airport official, who had arranged a meeting between my relatives and me at the airport. Soon after our hugs and greetings, he was curious about our little restless Anand. Without too much conversation, he quickly escorted us, bypassing the long waiting queue. From their facial expression, they did not approve our privileged treatment. Within thirty minutes, we were at the immigration office where my cousin explained our situation to get permission to take us out to the airport to the café area. He promised to be back at 6.00pm to escort us to board the plane for the 8.00pm take-off.

We were surprised to see the big crowd from Suba's side, together with my relatives, at the airport to say goodbye to us. I noticed my sister and her family had all travelled via bus to see me. They must have started their journey very early in the morning to meet us at the airport that afternoon. My aunty, her neighbours, and a few others whom I had only met briefly were there unexpectedly. Suba's uncles and aunties were there to greet us, as well as her brothers.

< 11 > The career plan that went wrong

Luckily, the airport was not too busy that day and there were several empty seats for all our older and frail visitors to be seated as we chatted. During that transit stop we managed to speak to all our visitors and guests. We, somehow, even managed with the few of Suba's relatives who were only able to converse in Malayalam and those who could only speak Tamil from my side of the family. My great effort to communicate to my families in Tamil made my nieces giggle at my accent. Several times I had to pause to search my brain for the appropriate Tamil words. Somehow, they understood the message that I wanted to share with them.

Most of the time Suba and I were answering similar questions about the new country that we were heading to. Several older relatives tried to convince us to return to Malaysia because they believed that Malaysia was the best country in the world. They shared their observations of graduates who had returned to settle in Malaysia after their overseas studies and had quickly moved to senior positions with good incomes.

My relatives were concerned about the availability of Indian cuisines in Australia. We had to assure them that multicultural Australia was very well catered to, include the special vegetarian needs of Indians. One other common question was about our long-term intention to settle in Australia. Suba responded that we had no idea what was waiting for us, but we had to keep our options open and apply our skills and knowledge to any work environment. When we explained that the employees were well paid with good working conditions in Australia, and that the child-minding services for working mothers in Australia were excellent, there was a sudden sadness in their faces. Perhaps they began to think that our return to Malaysia to settle would not happen, given all the better opportunities in Australia.

When we checked our watches, we did not realise that we had been talking non-stop with our relatives and had forgotten all about eating lunch. Suddenly, my cousin appeared to warn us that our conversation had to end in no less than thirty minutes. Immediately, there was a sudden silence and the crowd become melancholic. Several of our older relatives were already in tears, probably thinking they would not see us again. Hugs and kisses continued until my cousin had to physically move us from the teary crowd. They were grateful for our visit on our way to Australia. Suba and I felt very glad to have spent some quality time with them before heading to our destination. From that stopover, it was obvious that the affection for us from both families still remained very strong.

We passed through some checkpoints within the Malaysian airport and were in the "passengers only" area when they announced the boarding. Like our previous experience, we were allowed to board before the others. We thanked my cousin for his help at the stairway of the plane before entering.

We placed Anand in the provided basinet in the first row of the economy section. We were so relieved to be back in the plane, as for the last few hours at the KL Airport we had been very busy with our relatives and did not have a chance to relax. As the plane was about to be airborne, Suba quickly started breastfeeding Anand, and afterwards I saw the relief in Suba's face after she comforted Anand in his basinet to sleep.

< 11 > The career plan that went wrong

When the flight was airborne, we had our pre-dinner drinks. I took over Anand while Suba enjoyed her meal first. As Anand was relaxed and quiet, we dozed off until his noise woke us. From then on, he was restless and had to be held in our arms for most of the remaining journey.

Some of the passengers at the far end of the plane were yelling with joy as we crossed the Australian landmass. They were peering through the windows and pointing to the land below. I presumed many of the excited passengers were migrating, just like us. They were elated to see their future country and were full of hopes and dreams. We were glad to watch their excitement because it gave us a good feeling about our unknown destination. Unfortunately, Suba was not excited as she saw the barren land without the very tall buildings the UK had. She felt that Australia was far too backwards, whereas I felt it was the land of opportunities.

As soon as the plane came to a halt in Melbourne, several of the Melbourne-bound passengers left the plane while the others remained seated. About an hour later, we received the announcement that the plane was taking off to Sydney; around fifty percent of the passengers remaining in the economy section of the plane were Sydney-bound. Again, Anand was restless as the cabin pressure changed when the plane began to take off, but we knew that the next leg of our journey would be much shorter.

As we arrived at Sydney airport, I held Anand in a baby sling so that my hands were free to collect our luggage. The queue for entry visas was long and it took forty-five minutes to get our passports stamped before we were cleared by customs and had our luggage checked-in. We headed straight to the Sydney domestic terminal and also realised we had landed in the Australian summer. I had no time to change my clothes as we had only two hours before our next boarding, so we headed straight to the boarding gate. We were uncomfortable in our heavy clothes, unlike the rest of the passengers who were in light summer clothes. After we boarded, I held Anand in my arms as there was no basinet for him on this flight. Once again, he became restless with the cabin pressure changes and his cries drew attention from our fellow passengers. He became quiet again when Suba was feeding him, but his noise had attracted nearby passengers who started a conversation. A couple of them were curious to know our background and about our two-day journey to Australia. One particular passenger was very keen to share her knowledge about the Gold Coast and some of the interesting places we should visit once we had settled in Queensland. As we were new to the country, we made note of the advice. As the plane was nearing Brisbane, I felt the temperature rise. Several of the impatient passengers were already lifting their luggage from the cabin lockers above my head, despite the cabin staff's warnings. We did not move or undo our seatbelts because we were too tired, instead waiting for the plane to stop completely first.

‹ **12** ›

My first place to settle in Australia

The noise from our fellow passengers reaching for their luggage and clicking their seatbelts made me realise that the plane had completely stopped. As soon as the cabin doors were opened, I felt the ambient heat creeping into the plane. We collected our luggage and Anand's things before leaving the plane. We were very thankful of our fellow passengers who let us move forward in the queue as we walked down the stairs. As soon as we got off the plane, we felt the 31ºC heat. Little Anand remained restless because of the heat, pressure changes and his disturbed sleep pattern. Within twenty minutes we had our luggage and exited the airport.

Before long we noticed Faisal (Suba's older brother) and his close friend, Peter Ho, waving to us. Peter (also a PhD student) was around the same age as Faisal and of Chinese descent, from Hong Kong. They observed the tired looks on our faces and quickly helped us get into Peter's car that had been cooled for us with the engine running. The car's air-conditioner was enough to cool us, but we still felt sorry for our three-month-old son who was already restless and had become further unsettled on reaching Brisbane. As adults, Suba and I were totally exhausted by the end of the flights and we could understand how uncomfortable it was for Anand. The journey to Faisal's apartment took around forty minutes.

Arnie (Faisal's wife) and Ferlynda (Faisal's daughter) were waiting for us at their rental apartment in St Lucia, the closest suburb to the university. The second floor of the building had five apartments in a row, while the ground level was a carport. As their dwelling was close to the road it was easy to transfer our bags from the car to the second floor of the apartment through its winding staircase. We were lucky to have Peter and Faisal's help with the luggage so we could concentrate on Anand. Our things were placed in our room, as allocated by Faisal.

The apartment's basic facilities included a small kitchen with an oven, toaster, microwave, electric kettle and gas stove. We soon noticed some mosquitoes were waiting to welcome us as well. As soon as the windows were opened for some fresh air, the anxious guests rushed in to demonstrate their 'love bites'!

Arnie soon invited us for the first home-cooked meal in Australia. I remembered Arnie cooking delicious food in Glasgow when Faisal was an undergraduate student. I managed to have a quick, cold shower before the late lunch. After Suba's shower, Anand was given a quick bath to freshen him up. Suba and I felt relieved after the cold showers, changing into loose comfortable clothes before we indulged in the long-awaited Malaysian dishes. Soon after the sumptuous meal, followed by the chilled, fresh, ripe mangoes as our dessert, we were too tired to keep our eyes open. We rested for two hours before we heard Anand's cry.

When Suba attended to Anand, she quickly yelled for me with horror on her face. We could not believe what we saw! We soon realised the mistake we made using a disposable nappy. This was the only time we had used disposable, synthetic material on Anand and the sudden change from cold weather to hot temperature and the chemical reaction of the nappy must have caused his skin to peel off from his belly button and all the way down to his thighs, including his groin. The peeled area looked like a red mandarin, which made us very emotional. After a full feed, with a cool breeze from the table fan, we were glad to see him doze off to sleep on a clean cotton sheet.

We had not seen such a skin reaction like this caused by a disposable nappy. We felt guilty to have inflicted pain on our helpless baby. We discussed the possibility of taking him to the doctor, but ended up deciding to let him sleep and let the wound heal naturally. From my nursing experience with patients who had lost more than 50 percent of their skin through burns, skin problems like this were generally managed just by turning people constantly from their back to their front. We managed Anand similarly, and as his skin started to heal, we had to refrain him from scratching off the germinating, itchy skin.

That night we went back to sleep when Anand was settled, but we were up again at about 3am because our body clocks were still adjusting. When we felt the cool breeze coming through the windows, we could not resist taking a walk around the neighbourhood.

We admired the private, individual houses. We presumed that they must be wealthy as we noticed their brand-new cars next to their homes. Their grounds were well manicured with several tropical fruit trees, vegetable patches and shrubs with very colourful flowering plants, which made their yards look enchanting. Their well-trimmed, green lawns with bird baths and interspersed stone sculptures were elegant.

In between those private homes were apartments whose yards needed some attention. Several of those apartments had older-looking cars parked out the front. We assumed those places must be rented by the students, as the suburb was close to the University of Queensland.

We noticed that there were several Queenslander style homes standing on tall stilts with staircases in front of them. We assumed the air-filled space below the wooden floor must cool the place in winter and ventilate the house during the hot summer months. Making these houses more elegant were the large, colourful, tropical trees in their yards, such as the Flame- of-the-Forest and Jacaranda.

As the temperature was around 17°C that morning, every minute of our hour-long stroll refreshed us.

When we returned, we both waited to have breakfast with Faisal, Arnie and Ferlynda with their usual toast and cereal, as well as the additional surprise of mangoes that Arnie had reserved for us. The conversation about our trip with family stories at the breakfast table engrossed Arnie and Suba, who continued talking for several hours as Faisal and Ferlynda left the apartment. Around 9.00am the temperature was already 20°C. That day Faisal came home for lunch and was surprised to note that the two sisters-in-law had not changed out of their pyjamas because of their "chatter".

Not long after, Faisal and Arnie decided to take Suba to the city to show her around and treat her to lunch before returning. I agreed to stay back to look after Anand, who was still recovering from his severe nappy rash. I took my time having lunch after my morning shower, then fed him the expressed milk that Suba had put in the refrigerator. I also fell asleep with him because my body clock was still adjusting from Aberdeen time.

When everyone returned, they had more tropical fruit for us to enjoy in the warm Brisbane weather. It was no surprise that by 5.00pm, the dark clouds turned into heavy rainfall. I could not help but enjoy the falling rain on the small balcony of the apartment; the warm rainwater brought some scary lightning and thunder. The rain stopped within thirty minutes, but it had cooled me.

Over the next few days we relaxed and got to know the suburb of St Lucia, as well as Arnie and Faisal's circle of friends. One of the great social events they all engaged in was badminton at the games hall at the University of Queensland. The games were played indoors where it was convenient to bring babies and where children could sit and watch the games. As the new arrivals, Suba and I joined the social Sunday games. Andrew Menon, a Malaysian-born biochemist who worked full-time in pharmaceuticals, was a very generous and caring bachelor friend of Faisal's. He often dropped in to greet us, offering lifts for shopping and fetching us for badminton on Sundays.

Anand was usually placed in his buggy at the end of the hall while we enjoyed our games. I noticed the weekly training and coaching improved my fitness and performance. I was invited to play for the C Division in the University of Queensland team at the Chandler Complex in the Commonwealth Sports Stadium. Luckily, Andrew helped out with the one-hour trip as I had no car at the time.

One afternoon in 1982, Faisal and his friends invited us to join them for a weekend at Noosa beach. We all agreed to share expenses to keep the cost low, as we were all on limited income. We were having so much fun at the rented house until someone suggested we should take the opportunity to visit the nudist beach at Noosa. As a curious lot, we all agreed to visit as we returned to Brisbane. The visit ended up with a one-hour walk on a hot day to finally see the quiet beach with hardly any people, but some gorgeous high waves that I could not resist. Soon Peter jumped in to refresh himself as well.

As the waves came in, we both tried falling over the crests as they dragged us to the shore, but the currents changed and we were dragged back into the ocean. As we realised we were being dragged out further and could no longer feel the seabed, we panicked. Quickly, we started swimming to the shore. Although I was making progress, each time the waves came I was dragged further into the ocean. In my panic I kept my eyes open even though I had sand going into them. I tasted the salty water as it went through my nose and mouth. My swimming breathing technique I had learnt was soon forgotten in my alarm, but I did not stop swimming. For a moment I felt my brain say that I was drowning and should give up the struggle. Consciously, I agreed that I was fighting a losing battle and should give up. Mentally I had given up, and physically the only thing I was doing to survive was maintaining my strokes. I was exhausted and my strokes were slow but still rhythmic in my semi-conscious state. Luckily, the slowing ocean current brought me closer to the shore, about two metres. The others on the shore did not realise we were struggling in the water as they assumed that we were having fun.

Peter and I could not give enough thanks for the badminton training we'd had on the weekends. If we had not improved our fitness, we would not have been able to swim against such strong currents. Fortunately, neither of us had any muscle cramps that could have drowned us. We both thanked our coach Mr Svendson for his pedantic, rigorous training regime. That unforgettable near-drowning incident still remains with me whenever I am in the water, whether in the ocean or a safe swimming pool.

After several weeks, Suba and I talked about purchasing a second-hand car as the public transport in Brisbane was not suitable for our needs: taking Anand for his health checks, Suba doing the shopping and me searching for a job. At that time, I did not have an income except the small family allowance I received from the Australian Social Welfare Department fortnightly. I just had enough cash to cover my shared lodging and food expenses. I had some small savings from Scotland which I was hesitant to spend on my first car in

Australia, but at the same time I did not want to inconvenience my four-month-old son and Suba.

The purchase of second-hand, five-seater *Nissan Sunbird* assisted both families. I dropped Faisal at his laboratory in the morning and fetched him home in the evening. Sometimes Faisal volunteered to drive Anand around the block to help him fall asleep on his restless days. The vehicle was handy for us to visit Arnie and Faisal's friends whenever we managed to find time.

Suba was still a bit concerned about Australia as our new country. We were approaching our first Australian Christmas and the weather was very different, so everything felt very strange. Suba's attitude changed when Dr Peter Swanell (Faisal's supervisor) had a chat with her at a Christmas party at his house.

One day, we met Peter at the laboratory and he invited us to come along with Faisal to his Christmas party. When Suba was hesitant to go, I agreed to return home with her if she felt uncomfortable.

The party started at 11.00am and was soon in full swing and getting loud. Peter had cooked the traditional turkey, while others had brought along Asian dishes. Everyone was enjoying themselves with Peter's easy-going style without any formality. Several heads of departments and PhD students with their spouses were there as well. Peter's big home had several entertainment rooms with large verandas, which meant people were able to relax outside as well. We were busy eating while talking with Arnie and her friends about our days in Scotland, where the Christmas experience was different.

In Scotland, during Christmas, the grounds were usually covered with snow and the ambient temperature could easily drop down to minus 15°C. Some of those very familiar places soon became unidentifiable because they were completely covered with snow. The frozen water in the lakes and ponds in the parks became ideal skating grounds for children. The naked trees turned white with snow-covered tops. Despite the cold Scottish weather, the neighbourhoods were alive with decorations and coloured lights at night. People continued their fun outside their homes on icy surfaces. Christmas in Australia at Peter's place was different to Dundee because of the hot weather, but, fortunately, we did not feel the hot weather because of Peter's air-conditioning. Anand managed to fall asleep, which allowed us some free time to enjoy ourselves at the party. By the evening, the temperature had dropped from 35°C to 23°C and the party was coming to a close.

Suba and I were very grateful to Peter, who hardly knew us but invited us along to his home, which made a big difference to us. It was then that Peter understood our uncertainty about settling in Australia and advised us not to compare the lives we had in the UK with Australia as they were very different in many ways. He told us that the future opportunities in Australia were far greater than in the UK as he had lived in Manchester before Brisbane. He was very sincere in his advice and told us about his experiences to share his life examples. According to Peter, who had adapted to life in Australia, he had no regrets and, likewise, we stopped the comparisons and began to settle in Australia as our new country!

I soon realised that finding a job to match my education and experience was not easy in Brisbane. I applied for several advertised vacancies and was disappointed I was not short-listed. I soon gave up the idea of finding a position to match my qualifications.

As time passed, I felt anxious without a job and desperate to do something to earn an income. One afternoon, I received a note regarding my job application from an employer who wanted to drop in to see me at my place. I was excited to receive such a warm letter. Firstly, he had offered me a job and secondly, he wanted to meet me, making me even more excited. I was already waiting for him at the curb near the apartment as he got out of his car with a smile. Soon afterwards he pointed to the bundled papers and magazines in his boot and the further piles in the back seat of his car. When he explained the number of advertising material I had to deliver within two days for a small wage, my enthusiasm disappeared. Yes, I was desperate for a job and prepared to do anything that could give me a decent wage, but not three thousand catalogues that had to be delivered within two days for a payment of $30! Well, as there was no other offer coming my way, I had to take up the job until I found something better. I reassured myself that it would keep me occupied and improve my physical fitness because of the walking I had to do to deliver them. However, my decision to accept the job was too prompt, because I did not consider the tropical summer rains in Brisbane.

I started the delivery that same afternoon and I finished it as agreed. Some days I began delivery at 4.00am, before it became too hot in the afternoon. Sometimes, the dogs would frighten me from going near letter boxes and on other days the heavy morning rains made my walks a bit harder with the load of paper in my hand. Sometimes, I had a tarpaulin to cover the papers when it rained. The only benefit from that experience was learning the suburb of St Lucia. I admired those amazingly elegant houses with swimming pools and other outdoor activities for the families. I also began to dream about owning a similar house one day. It was a lovely, cost-free dream at that time because I had no money and no job to support my family. Those aspirations and dreams frustrated me and made me more determined to improve my status as soon as I could. I consoled myself by saying that these difficult times were temporary and would not be there forever.

After eight weeks in Australia, I was still doing the catalogue delivery two days a week for a few dollars, which was only enough to pay for a family meal at a restaurant. Suba decided to start work at Wesley Hospital on weekends while I looked after Anand. The night shift duty suited her because she was able to join family events during the day. When I drove Suba to work about 9.00pm, I had to take Anand along because I could not leave him alone at home unless Arnie or Faisal were there. When he woke up in the middle of the night, I fed him expressed milk that had been stored in the refrigerator. In the morning when we waited at the hospital to fetch Suba, Anand would get excited as soon as he saw her walking towards the car. Although he was strapped to a child chair in the rear seat, he would struggle to free himself to go to Suba. Suba, who was fully aware of his impatience, therefore always had a shower post work before getting into the car next to him. I often waited until he had his first few minutes of frenzy feeding before I drove the car. It was an amazing event to watch him suckle in such a hurry as if he had been starved for days. As he continued to feed, he would slow down and give his mum a satisfied smile.

At the time I was unable to find a proper job until I was shortlisted to work with Australian Mutual Provident (AMP). AMP was one of the largest insurance companies in Australia with offices and branches in every Australian capital city. I was interviewed among a few other graduates and experienced people at the Brisbane headquarters and was soon notified that I was successful and would be stationed at AMP Toowong (a town between St Lucia and Brisbane). I was pleased that I did not have to go into the city centre and pay for the parking there. The new, comfortable office with a computer, personal telephone and access to photocopying, faxes and ample free parking spaces enticed me to accept the position. I liked the weekly fixed wages while training and the lack of physical labour.

I was surprised to find out that a few very successful agents were earning more than a million dollars working only three days a week. The remaining two days they played golf with their friends while the office administration was managed by their personal assistants. While they were enjoying their golf, they also signed up new clients from the golf course, who often ended up as good, reliable customers.

My situation as a new recruit was challenging because I hardly knew the local community and had trouble finding the addresses of new clients. Despite the challenges, I kept going as I needed the income. Our combined earnings were just enough to pay the 50 percent contribution for the shared accommodation and food costs.

Six months after our arrival, Faisal submitted his thesis and packed his things to return to Malaysia. Suba and I were sad as we had stayed together in the same apartment for six months in cramped conditions and we would miss them. That morning I left for work late after saying goodbye, but the sorrowful thoughts of their farewell were still in my mind at work.

That same day, I had a surprise call from Andrew when I was just about to finish work at 7.00pm. He urgently wanted to discuss the prospects of buying a house. I was a bit hesitant as I knew I did not have any cash and our earnings were just enough to cover our house expenses. Furthermore, my position as an insurance agent did not guarantee a constant income and was very much dependent on the number of sales I did each month.

On Andrew's insistence, I agreed to go with him to visit a real estate manager. At the time I felt frustrated living in the second floor of the St Lucia apartment as Anand was crawling and attempting to walk. Both of us felt that Anand would soon learn how to open the front door of the second floor, which was too close to an unprotected staircase. Suba and I had already decided to move out to a safer place at any cost so that Anand's gross motor skills could develop as normal.

That night, the manager of Hooker Homes in Brisbane advised us to look at the last few available houses in the suburb of Centenary before we progressed with any further discussions. The next evening, Andrew and I visited the suburb after work and were excited about the prospect of buying two of those houses. We knew very well that we had no savings! In the interim, I checked with several banks and building societies for a loan, but all of them demanded a minimum 20 percent deposit. At that time in 1983, the property market was booming and housing costs were escalating quite rapidly. Houses that were $30000 had quickly risen to $60000 over a six-month period.

At the second long discussion about finances, the agent said bluntly that Andrew and I definitely did not qualify for borrowing money from any lenders. He suggested we meet a manager he knew from the loan section with Citicorp Finance Company. He was happy to arrange the meeting for us, but did not guarantee any positive outcome for a loan unless we could convince Citicorp.

Both of us realised we had nothing to lose and we should have a go at the offered opportunity. We understood that we had to act as wealthy people and as if we would have no problem repaying the loan. I was determined to use this one opportunity to break my cycle from renting to owning. We agreed to meet the Citicorp decision-maker for our loans at the bar where he usually drank on Friday evenings. As planned, Andrew and I turned up at the bar wearing our full suits just a few minutes before the decision-maker and his team came. Upon seeing us, the manager quickly introduced us to the team as planned.

After the brief introduction, Andrew and I checked our pockets and managed to buy them their drinks. As advised by the manager, we pretended to be busy and wealthy, and we talked up ourselves. After thirty minutes of chatting, the friendly finance decision-maker said that lending us the money should be fine, but we would attract a high interest rate. As soon as we heard his verbal endorsement for our loans, both of us excused ourselves from the group as we had no money to buy them another round of drinks for them or even for ourselves.

As we were driving home, Andrew and I were very pleased that we had impressed the "gatekeeper" to offer us our loans, but we still needed a minimum 5 percent deposit for a loan at 21 percent interest!

Within two weeks we received a letter saying the loan to purchase our first home had been approved by Citicorp. The lender was happy to approve the loan because we agreed to pay the high interest rate of 21 percent, which startled some of my friends.

Suba and I were excited to note that the government grant application was approved, but we were disappointed to note that we would only receive $1500, leaving us $1000 short. I heard several other applicants in similar situation had obtained more than $3000. Although we would have preferred to receive more money from the government, we were grateful for the amount we did get. When I collected all of our money for the deposit, I was still short and did not reach the $3250 I needed. With the approval of the manager, I moved into the new house before the settlement took place, so I had rent-free accommodation for two months, which helped us reach the required minimum deposit.

We felt special as the proud owners of a new house, but we were in no position to purchase any other essentials for the house. It took us two months to buy a washing machine and refrigerator. It took us nearly a year to replace the blankets in the windows with curtains. As the yard had no shade from the trees, we had insulation put in the attic within the first six months. We slept on the floor for six months until we bought a king-size bed. The flyscreens, built-in cupboards and the backyard landscaping to drain off the water, took us a few years.

As the new home owners we were happy, but, somehow, had to maintain the monthly loan repayments. Most of the money we earned from part-time work covered the loan repayment and we hardly had anything left for other expenses. We both limited our spending where we could. Suba took meals from home to her night shifts twice a week. Similarly, I took sandwiches to work and limited myself from eating outside, but occasionally I had to join my workmates for lunch where I kept my spending to the absolute minimum. We did not go out to restaurants, the cinema or even spend money on fast food. Most of the time our home-cooked meals, lasted us for two to three days, thus saving money from eating outside. Sales were great opportunities to purchase our household white goods, using credit cards. I was not a great gardener, but my small vegetable patch grew enough of my favourite hot chillies and eggplants. I also had some other fresh produce that helped us during our tight budget days.

While we were still managing our situation as new parents and enjoying our status as new house owners, I was constantly looking for a full-time position where I could use my qualifications and experience.

In October 1983, I was offered the position of Nurse Educator at Princess Alexandra Hospital (PAH) in the School of Nursing, which had twenty-five teaching staff. The nursing students were prepared for registration in general nursing with the Queensland Registration Board. In those days, Australian hospitals had their own schools that trained nurses for their state registrations. As there was no national registration board, the training hospital had their own curriculum to prepare them for the State Board examination, which they had to pass before they were allowed to practise.

The hospitals at the time had very strict policies on uniforms, conduct and taking sick leave etcetera. Even during lectures, the male educators had to wear short sleeved white shirts with green epaulettes and long white pants with white or brown shoes. The male nursing students wore the same uniform, but without the epaulettes. The female educators had to wear white dresses with green epaulettes. The female nursing students had to wear white tops and skirts with tights. The students' shoes had to be white. The six sets of uniforms for all staff and students were supplied and laundered by the hospital, which was a big help, especially for me because it saved me from washing and ironing my uniforms.

After starting work at PAH, I felt my self-esteem improving because my knowledge and skills were valued, and I also had quality time with my family soon after work. I was glad to leave home to start work at 7.15am and be home by 4.30pm to spend time with my family during the week. The senior position's wage improved our living conditions.

My ability to teach science and how it applied to the practice of nursing across the three years of training was well acknowledged by students and staff. Soon I was promoted to team leader for first-year educators. The promotion made me responsible for supervising all first-year educators and all issues related to the first year of the course.

My routine in Brisbane involved working from Monday to Friday, while Suba worked regularly on Friday and Saturday nights. As Anand was still under two years old, we ensured that at least one of us was with him and he was never left alone. There were times when I felt very uncomfortable transferring him into the car during his deep sleep as I could not leave him home alone when I took Suba to work at night. Suba caught the train to work and back, but I still had to drop her at Darra Station, about fifteen minutes by car from the house.

One Saturday morning, Anand and I were waiting for Suba to arrive from work and Suba was nowhere to be seen. I panicked when I could not see her at the station at the usual time. Anand was normally asleep, but on that particular day he was anxiously waiting for his important "milk lady". That morning, I had to sit next to him and calm him until the next train arrived, but Suba did not arrive on that one either. I began to worry about all the things that could have gone wrong! I had to go home to ring the hospital and I was told that she had left work at the usual time. My heart was thumping and I was not quite sure what to do next. Anand recognised my anxiety and knew that something was not right. We returned to the station and I carried him in my arms as he wanted to know where his mum had gone. Suddenly, Suba appeared; as we were driving home Suba explained how she was so tired she fell asleep on the train and missed her usual stop.

I was enjoying my work at PAH School of Nursing in planning, writing examination questions, marking all the first-year examinations and supporting new educators. My science degree had definitely provided me the knowledge to explain the basic sciences and how they applied to nursing practice.

I was enjoying my work and spending all my free time with my young family. One evening, when I was playing with Anand at home, Suba had a call from my oldest brother Krish, which surprised us. Suba and I knew that he did not want to have any contact with us since our wedding seven years ago. His message was to inform me that my mother was critically ill and if I wanted to see her alive, I should go to Malaysia as soon as possible. At the time I heard of my mum's serious illness, I was very upset, but also quite heavily in debt because I had just purchased several whitegoods for the house with my credit card. Luckily, I still had enough on one of my cards to pay for my flights and other needs for the trip to Malaysia. At the time of the urgent call, Suba was confirmed pregnant with our second child and was still working part-time.

When my Education Superintendent heard that I had to go, she was not happy for me to leave work with such short notice. She expected me to ask for leave in writing, which could have taken several days. I felt I did not have time to wait and was prepared to face the consequences on my return. I was aware that my departure without permission could end in a dismissal from work.

At the time, Krish had five children with the oldest sixteen years old and the rest much younger. All five children were attending school and the house was also busy with regular visitors related to his work. As he had his own civil engineering practice and a large family, life was very busy for him.

On arriving in Malaysia, that same evening Krish took me to the hospital to visit my mum. My bedridden mother recognised me as soon as I walked into her two-bed unit. She barely had any clothes on and I was appalled to see her in that situation, especially in a private hospital. When I compared the care given to my mother with my patients at PAH, my mother's care was far worse. I felt sorry for Krish who had to pay enormous hospital costs with the hope that she was getting the best treatment. Following my discussion with him, Krish realised that the money he was paying for the hospital did not match the expected quality of care given to my mum.

Within the next two days, Krish decided to bring Mum home. She was accommodated in the prayer room which was close to the toilet and shower facilities. After a couple of days at Krish's place, I returned to fetch Suba and Anand and came again to say goodbye to my mum before returning to Australia. Unfortunately, when we were about to leave, we heard my mother had passed away. I quickly changed my date of return and came to Krish's house without Suba, as she was pregnant and not very comfortable attending my mother's funeral with our two-year-old.

By the time I arrived, many of our closest relatives from

all around the country had also arrived. At the funeral the next day, all of my siblings were there except for my brother Maniam. My mother's body was dressed beautifully and laid in a coffin in the living room where everyone could see her. Her body was kept chilled with dry ice because the temperature in Malaysia was usually around 37ºC and could decompose the body easily. Insects were kept away by the lighted oil lamps and incense.

As I watched her, it brought back faint memories about the troubles my mother had to handle without a husband to manage the six of us. Although she had lived her life as an uneducated woman, her efforts to educate us had been amazing. She must have faced numerous challenging circumstances to raise us. She had been very proud of us, but did not live long enough to enjoy the returns of her hard work.

The funeral criers started the mourning as people arrived and the decorated funeral van was waiting, but there was still no sign of my brother, Maniam! All the grandchildren were around her body holding lighted wicks as a mark of respect and all the sons were in a white *dothi* with no shirts. As we were about to finish the last rites, my brother Maniam appeared in the nick of time to join us. Soon after her body was lifted into the funeral van, the loud cries from everyone went up to express their condolences. Quickly, all the closest males followed the funeral van to the crematorium, which was about five kilometres away. The crematorium staff cremated the body and we collected the ashes and drove to the nearest beach, which was about twenty kilometres away, to disperse them in the ocean, as was the Hindu custom.

On my return to Faisal's house the next day, I narrated the funeral to my brother-in-law and Suba as we prepared our return journey to Australia. I was a bit anxious when I returned to work because of the strict PAH protocols that I had not followed. I made an appointment with my boss to explain the circumstances I faced while in Malaysia at my mother's funeral. All the senior hospital staff and School of Nursing staff understood my sorrowful time and supported my grieving period. Memories of my mum did come back to me because I still missed her, but life had to go on!

When we were back in Brisbane, Suba continued her weekend work during her pregnancy. We managed to do activities as a family when she woke up from her few hours of sleep, following her night shifts.

One particular evening, Suba had pregnancy pains as I was leaving for my weekly badminton game and I had some reservations as there was no one at home to help her if she went into labour. Not long afterwards, while I was at the game, our friend Andrew arrived at 9.00pm with Anand. He had seen Suba just before coming and advised me to return because she was in serious pain and her contractions were escalating. Luckily, Anand was very fond of Andrew and was happy to stay with him. Without any hesitation, I left my game for home to take Suba to the hospital.

As soon as I reached home, I made sure Suba was ready to leave for the Royal Women's Hospital in Brisbane at once. As soon as she was admitted to hospital, she was taken to the delivery room. I managed to stay with her in the labour suite in the emergency department. At that stage

< 12 > My first place to settle in Australia

I was not sure whether she would go into delivery without delay because Anand was delivered well after twenty-four hours of waiting. Surprisingly, at 11.24pm a baby girl was delivered without any complications, as we had hoped. I thanked God for the easy and uncomplicated delivery of a healthy baby girl who we named Anuja. After the hugs to my newborn girl, I had to say goodbye and leave the mother and daughter in hospital.

After Anuja's arrival, Suba had to stay in hospital and I had a challenging time with my full-time work while attending to Anand. At that time, we were still new in the country and did not know anyone close enough to ask for help. Andrew, who we had known for a year, had already been very helpful to us. Even prior to the delivery he had helped to take Suba to maternity clinic appointments for check-ups as I was unable to due to the strict hospital rules.

On the days I had to deliver my lectures, Andrew managed to babysit Anand until I finished the key teaching sessions and then quickly rushed back to pick him up from Andrew's house. By the time I reached Andrew's place, it was almost past midday and often Andrew was delayed in going to work. After fetching Anand, I had to cook his steamed vegetable lunch, and I also did some Asian dishes to take for Suba.

We would get to the hospital by 5.00pm as that was the first visiting time. Anand would spend a few moments with Suba and Anuja as soon as we were allowed in. We both had to leave when the bell was rung after an hour. We stayed outside in the hospital grounds for the next visiting time at 7.30pm. Meanwhile, I allowed Anand to play in the park near the hospital, fed him before we visited Suba and Anuja the second time.

Anand was not happy to leave his mum or his sister when we had to go home. I was equally sad to leave the hospital. At that time, I felt very lonely as there was no one from our families to share the joy of our second child. I felt very sad for Suba as she had no visitors at the bedside like the other new mums in the ward. We were aware that we had to face such sad circumstances because we had chosen to leave our families to come abroad to start a new life in a new country. If Suba was in Malaysia, there would have been quite a number of people visiting her and taking turns to be around her and to help us. They would have celebrated the arrival of our new baby. Anand would also have been cared for by one of our relatives, which would have eased the stress on us. The Malaysian culture of support from extended family was definitely missed!

After a week, Suba was discharged from hospital. Meanwhile, I modified my home routine to suit my full-time work so that I could spend time with my two young children. On weekdays, I often got up around 5.00am and did some gardening for about thirty minutes, before I went for a three-kilometre run around the suburb and was home from work by 4.15pm to spend time with my young family.

As the Brisbane weather was warm on most days (except in winter), we were able to spend our quality time in our yard or at nearest public park. Sometimes Suba joined us after she had organised our dinner.

Once Anuja began walking, the weekends were equally

busy for the three of us. We would go to the Brisbane City Library fairly early in the morning while Suba was catching up on her sleep from her night shift. We often stopped at the parks to watch the birds or to play on the swings or seesaws before returning home. Those evenings we would end up playing around the house in our yard before washing, dinner and bed.

As a new father, my intention was to keep the children physically active and socially motivated with an inquisitive mind. I taught them to question and understand why things happened in nature, how plants grew, why animals killed each other for food, etcetera. When I recalled my younger days, I had no one to guide my learning. As I had lost my dad at four years old, I had no paternal love or guidance. At school I ended up under my oldest brother's guidance and his very poor communication skills often caused fear in me. I wanted my children to enjoy their childhood and grow up learning with fun and without fear.

Suba and I often encouraged both of them to read and discuss issues they were interested in, and guided them to seek the answers rather than providing them. From a very early age of three, we cultivated their reading habits and encouraged them to find the answers to their own questions. We created fun in learning things by themselves. Sometimes we used the microscopes in the town library to look at small animals, or watched videos or did quizzes at home as a family. I still treasure that quality time with my two children.

When Anand turned three, he was ready to go to kindergarten, which was only about five hundred metres from our home. We only had one car that I used for work, so Suba would walk Anand to and from kindergarten while pushing Anuja in the buggy. Anand loved to show his school work and spend time talking to Anuja about what he did at kindergarten. Sometimes he got frustrated when Anuja was not concentrating on what was being said.

My arriving home after work freed Suba to finish the dinner preparations. Apart from the brain activities with them, I also did physical work out in the yard: ball games, running around and somersaulting until both of them were quite tired. Occasionally, we muddied ourselves in the homemade sandpit. I was not concerned if they were dirty or messed up their clothes, the fun we had was more important. Hosing water on each other before their wash was the last activity before dinner.

Their informal learning even continued during their wash times, and sometimes Suba joined us. As we were bathing, we had many interesting questions from Anand and Anuja about our bodies. Soon after washing, we were in our pyjamas and ready for dinner as a family. At the dining table, Anand was on a high chair while Anuja was fed by both of us. By the time they finished their meals they would be falling asleep because they'd had too much fun with their physical activities!

When they went to bed, they enjoyed us reading to them before they fell asleep. Sometimes the bedtime reading could go on for more than an hour and we would have fallen asleep before them in their bed. Once they were in bed, Suba and I would watch television with a glass of wine each. Some nights we had cries from Anuja, who would end up sleeping in our bed.

While we were enjoying our settling in the country we

< 12 > My first place to settle in Australia

now called home, we also thought about our friends, Angie and Gana, who were still living in Aberdeen. Ever since we left the U.K, we had been in constant contact with them to keep them informed, as promised, of what was happening with us in "our new country". I kept them informed about the vast opportunities for nurses in Australia. I was still working as a Nurse Educator at the PAH and saw similar opportunities.

I suggested Gana commence his registration process with the Queensland Nurse Registration Board while he still was in the UK. Initially, Gana was reluctant but, after some persuasion, he decided to do it. I suggested to Angie and Gana to treat the trip as a holiday and if they felt that they did not like the country, they could return to the UK as they already had their permanent residency status there.

Fortunately, Gana was convinced, not only with my advice, but advice from his colleague who had successfully settled in Australia. Within three months of our conversation Gana was registered with the Psychiatric Nurse Register in Queensland and was given a permanent residence (PR) status directly from the UK before coming to Australia. I sponsored Gana and Angie for their PR in Australia and they were lucky because at that time of their application, the recruitment for overseas qualified nurses in Australia was very much in demand and therefore their visas were processed within six months.

Suba and I were pleased for them and looked forward to their arrival. We both knew that they would be employed quickly because of their experience. By the time they arrived in Australia in 1984, Gana had eleven years' experience in psychiatric nursing, while Angie had ten years' experience in theatre nursing. As they did not have any children, their travel would be less stressful.

We fetched them from the airport and had a welcome party at our house. Gana, who had become accustomed to the British way of life, enjoyed his drinks and parties. Some of his ex-colleagues, who had worked with him in Scotland, turned up for the welcome party at my place. Their conversations about lifestyle differences in the UK and Australia were informative for Gana.

After a month of relaxing in Brisbane, Angie and Gana explored their employment possibilities. At the time, I was an educator at PAH and happened to know the Psychiatric Superintendent there very well, who was in desperate need of a psychiatric nurse with relevant experience. One day, he asked if I knew any suitable psychiatric nurses for his department. I mentioned Gana and his experience, and soon after the conversation the superintendent scheduled Gana for a formal interview. Following the referee reports, Gana commenced a full-time position in the Psychiatry Division of PAH. Suba and I were very glad that at least one of them had started drawing a full-time income, although we were happy to accommodate them in our house until they found a place of their own. As we were working at the same hospital, we travelled to work together in my car.

After a month they wanted their own transport, so they purchased their first car in Australia. In the following two months they inspected a few new houses on the market before they bought their first home, which was only about three hundred metres away from ours. By then Gana had already been appointed as permanent staff at the hospital and his home loan approval was also guaranteed, which made his purchase hassle-free. Just before they moved into their new home, Angie was also employed full-time at the Wesley Private Hospital in the operating suite.

Both our families regularly visited each other and celebrated many occasions together. My children became regular visitors to Gana's new place and they were often dropped back by Gana following their dinner. Sometimes the children followed Suba for their evening walks to visit them. On several occasions Gana and Angie readily volunteered to look after the two children when we attended community functions.

My performance at work was very much appreciated by the Superintendent for Education. She never hesitated to praise my work and innovative teaching styles publicly at staff meetings. Although I only had five years of service at the school, she recommended me for a scholarship to study at the Queensland Institute of Technology (later the Queensland University of Technology). The twelve-month, full-time Postgraduate Diploma in Education was extremely relevant to the work I did as nurse educator. The scholarship provided me twelve months away from work with full salary to attend the university. Apart from the newly added qualification, I was also appointed to the Board of Nursing Studies Examination Panel of Queensland. The prestigious appointment meant I was expected to write the examination questions for the Nurses Registration Board of Queensland.

‹ **13** ›

Making my first brave move: Brisbane to Sydney

My work at PAH was going smoothly while Suba was enjoying her weekend work and our children were going well. On occasion Suba talked about her younger brother, Suresh, and her adopted sister, Sunitha. Suba was concerned about their welfare as they were under Raji's care after her mother passed away. Suba, as the only other female member of the family, had often thought about assisting them.

Suba and I were aware that Suresh and Sunitha were very different. On my return visit to Malaysia after my wedding, I had seen Suresh again. He still remained quiet and very reserved, with low self-esteem, and even though he was a teenager, he was still shy and seldom spoke to strangers. His command of the English language was very limited. He often came across as a reserved person with poor interpersonal skills. Sunitha, on the other hand, who was four years younger than Suresh, was an extrovert. She maintained her high self-esteem

< 13 >   Making my first brave move: Brisbane to Sydney

with good interpersonal communication skills. They were both emotionally affected by the loss of Suba's mother.

Suba and I often discussed about how to bring them over so that they would have better opportunities than in Malaysia. When I visited them last, I had spoken to them about migrating to Australia to live with us. From their body language I thought they were keen about coming but unsure of the new place. Furthermore, they hardly knew me.

Suba and I were more concerned about Suresh's future because he struggled academically and his education would come to a halt unless he had extra support. Sunitha had not yet started her secondary education and was quite promising, but again she needed help to maximise her potential, something the better education system in Australia could provide.

When I was thinking about helping them, I also reflected on my past circumstances and how my interest in study was hindered because of a lack of financial support. I told myself that I should not hesitate to give a helping hand to those who faced similar circumstances. At that time, I was in a position to help them as education was free in Australia. The only additional expenses for us would be their food and lodging. We decided they had to eat whatever we cooked for the family, whilst the accommodation had to be shared in the best possible way in our three-bedroom house.

Following our decision to bring them to Australia, we had some lengthy discussions with both Raji and Faisal, who were very supportive of the idea. I had to speed up the process to bring them to Australia because Suresh could become ineligible if he turned eighteen. After several months, I was glad to hear that they both were called for medical assessment by the Australian Embassy. We were confident that their legal documents would be soon approved for their travel.

One day, we received the awaited call from Raji to say that the flights had been booked and they would arrive in Australia within a few weeks. Suba was keen to help them, but also apprehensive of the household dynamics because there would be two extra people living with us permanently. We were both aware that the freedom we had would diminish when they joined us. At the same time, our primary interest was to assist them both for a brighter future. Suba and I discussed the additional costs related to their education and living expenses and how we would manage them. We briefed Anand and Anuja about them and how they were related to us so that they understood that they were part of our family. We also talked to them about the reshuffle of the rooms before their arrival. Anand, who was three years old, was able to comprehend what we were saying, while Anuja was just over a year old and listened very intently, but we were not sure how much she understood.

As planned, we prepared the day's lunch early before leaving to fetch them from the international airport in Brisbane. We left both our children with Gana and Angie to fetch the "new immigrants".

Upon arrival, Suresh and Sunitha were very quiet and only responded to questions as we drove them from the airport to our home. Soon after their wash and change, we called them to join us for the home-cooked lunch that we had prepared that morning. Suba and I made every effort to welcome them,

< 13 > Making my first brave move: Brisbane to Sydney

but as they struggled to communicate, because we were practically strangers to them. So it was difficult for us as it was for them. The first time they had seen me was at my wedding and they'd hardly had time to get to know me.

Suba was also a stranger, as she had been away in the UK when Sunitha was adopted. Suresh was comfortable with Suba, but Sunitha was not. Our main objective for them on their first day in Brisbane was to let them rest after the long journey and follow up with the orientation later.

The next morning, we sat for breakfast together, but there was hardly any conversation at the table. I could not speak Malayalam, and while Suresh and Sunitha could converse between themselves, they did not utter a word unless there was a question from Suba or me. I spoke to them in English about what Suba and I did for work and the reasons why we had chosen to settle in Australia. We shared some of the immigration challenges we went through to bring them into the country. I also explained about my limited income, most of which went to the house loan repayment, while Suba's part-time income supported the household expenses. At the end of the month when the electricity, house rates, bills and other expenses were paid, there was very little cash left to manage other expenses. We shared our financial situation very openly with them so that they understood the need to be conscious about the unnecessary wastage of water, food and electricity. We also told them that most of the items for the house were bought when there were sales at reduced price outlets. At this time Suresh was sixteen and Sunitha was twelve, so they understood what was being said.

Anand and Anuja accepted them as their new relatives following our introductions. Both of them overcame their initial shyness with the two strangers the next day.

Suba showed Sunitha and Suresh around the home where things were kept. Sunitha was uneasy because she realised that she was going to live with strangers and there would be less opportunity for a one-on-one relationship, like the one she'd had with Suba's mum before she passed away. Sunitha was glad to have her own room, whereas Suresh liked privacy and chose to use the garage which was converted into a bedroom. We were glad with his choice because the single-car garage was hardly used and we had an unused single bed with a mattress and a wardrobe stored there. He was aware that the garage would give him full privacy, but had no other facilities, so he had to share the shower, toilet and laundry in the house. Anand and Anuja had agreed to share a room to create space, whereas Suba and I kept the master bedroom.

From the day of their arrival, we had observed their eating habits and table manners, which were appropriate in Malaysia, but not for Australia. They were unfamiliar with the accepted eating habits and, just like me when I first went to Scotland, they had to be shown. We educated them on the expected Western table manners. We coached them on how to use a fork and knife to eat. I told them that personally I enjoyed eating curry and rice with my fingers, but in public I was expected to use cutlery. We advised them to avoid the Malaysian habits of slurping drinks or chewing with their mouths open. Suba reinforced that she also had to go through these cultural adjustments when she first moved to Scotland.

< 13 > Making my first brave move: Brisbane to Sydney

After a few days, Suba and I emphasised the importance of education for their future career paths. Despite our financial situation, we promised to support them in their education. I promised them that I was prepared to support them until they finished their tertiary studies in whatever discipline they preferred. We were not surprised that they had not thought about being a professional or graduate. Although Suresh had completed his junior high school education, he still did not know what career path he wanted to follow after his high school studies. His immediate response was that he wanted to be an engineer, which did not surprise me, because his two older brothers (Raji and Faisal) were in the engineering discipline.

Although I knew he was not an academically inclined student, I did not want to deny his interest in his engineering ambition, so I enrolled him in a high school to repeat his Year 9 studies. After spending a few stressful days at the high school, he soon realised that he would not be able to cope with academic studies, particularly mathematics. The next option was to enrol him into a Technical and Further Education (TAFE) institution in a Certificate of Business Studies in South Brisbane. He felt he could cope with this, but still needed some support from us. We were glad that he was finally settled into a course that would lead him to a professional career. Suresh was pleased the classes were only three evenings a week, and he was happy to attend them using public transport, although occasionally I fetched him after class.

Sunitha, on the other hand, was twelve years old and

had to continue her secondary education. After searching for a place in a few schools, she was enrolled in Year 7 at Indooroopilly State High School, which was an hour on the public bus. We were lucky that the bus stop was only a five-minute walk from the house and came every hour. She often had company in the bus with several other students. Going to school and returning home with her friends gave us a feeling of her safety, especially as she was new in the country.

Although I was very busy with my work and home, I always allocated time to check their school work. They understood that they both had to pull up their socks in order to keep up with their studies, and they followed the study schedule I set for them. They both had challenges with written and spoken English, which was understandable, as they came from Malay-speaking schools. Suresh's English was poorer than Sunitha's because he had did his previous study in Malay. Although the TAFE English was quite rudimentary, it was still challenging for Suresh. As the TAFE study was his first enrolment in Australia, we wanted his confidence to improve with good results. Suba and I spent hours coaching him with his English, which was his poorest subject. Although I came home tired from work, I kept up with the agreement to check their school work on a regular basis. It was very challenging for me and Suba to keep an eye on their studies as we had children of our own who needed attention as well! So, I had to manage the house rules with everyone's education as the top priority, while helping to keep the house tidy and sharing the housework and also having family fun together whenever possible.

< 13 > Making my first brave move: Brisbane to Sydney

It took about three months for Suresh and Sunitha to be comfortable with their study routines and to manage their studies with less attention from Suba and me. However, they had a very poor relationship with each other because of childhood sibling rivalries, which began to resurface in Brisbane. Sometimes there were outbursts of anger from both of them. Their yelling and screaming with physical violence did not help Anand and Anuja, who were much younger and watched their drama. I had to intervene at times to stop their remarks and subsequent aggressive behaviours towards each other. Despite these outbursts, there were peaceful, enjoyable moments for all, despite the occasional sibling rivalry.

The house was busy in the mornings as several of us had to leave for our own daily schedules. Suba walked Anand to school, Sunitha took the bus to her classes and I drove to work. Suresh slept in as his classes were in the evening.

In the evenings, I was usually home by 4.15pm and Suresh only had classes for three days a week and the rest of the time he was free too. We thought of capitalising on the free time we had by starting a business to earn a few extra dollars. We decided on a fish and chips shop. At the time I had no money, but my business partner was willing to loan me money at a low interest rate. I invested $15000 of borrowed money into the business, while three other partners invested another $15000 each. All four partners agreed that Suresh was to be the manager while the two other partners would help him as needed. We agreed to work there during our free time. Suresh had two days available for the business during the week and I had two days free on the weekends. The other two partners were a husband and wife who had different days off from work to help. Our fish and chips business venture was very exciting to start with, but our dreams to make money did not eventuate because none of us had sound business knowledge or experience in Australia. After twelve months of hard work, all of the business partners agreed to close the business; luckily, we maintained our friendship.

On reflection, there were several things that led to our business failure. The location of the business was at least thirty minutes from my house and I rushed to the business after my full-time work at 4pm. As Suresh did not have his own vehicle, he was dependent on the use of the partner's car, which prevented him in going to the business earlier or as he wanted. The pet shop next door to the business became an issue as well, as the smell of dead animals and animal droppings reached our premises. We overestimated Suresh's verbal communication skills; many times, he did not fully understand when taking a customer's order. Also, our decision to make him manager was a mistake, as he was fairly new to the Australian culture and was still learning about it. Finally, the twelve months of ongoing stress for all business partners ended when we jointly agreed to give the business away. Although we lost our investment, which was a painful, expensive experience, I was relieved to spend more quality time with my children on weekends and after work.

One day, I realised that I had been in the same position for more than seven years and needed a career change. I had been enjoying my position as a senior member of the hospital hierarchy, but where was I heading? Suba and I had a long

< 13 > Making my first brave move: Brisbane to Sydney

discussion that day, which continued well into the night, and we finally agreed that I needed a change. Returning to the clinical arena did not attract me because I had not done any "hands on" work for at least eight years. The second option was to move into tertiary teaching, which sounded more along my interests but required a postgraduate qualification, which needed to be considered carefully, given my poor financial position.

My interest in postgraduate study started when I thought about my future prospects. From my perspective as a qualified nurse and science graduate, I had fully used my science knowledge to teach nurses, and I felt the hunger for further knowledge to apply within the health care industry. At that time, nurse education was about to move to the tertiary sector and I had an ambition to be a lecturer but lacked a postgraduate qualification which was a pre-requisite for those positions. At the time in the late 1980s, there were limited postgraduate courses available for nurses in Australia. Among the few that were offered, there was a twelve-month course I was interested in: a Master of Nursing Administration course at the University of New South Wales in Sydney.

Suba and I talked over the challenges and how we could cooperatively manage them, so I could pursue my postgraduate study. The sacrifices we had to make would be huge and the returns were not certain. Suba was prepared to support me with the risk that I was taking and also support the family through the hassles during my study. When I discussed my idea with Gana, he was shocked, because he knew that my position at PAH was permanent and secure. He felt that I had a very good chance to be the Director of Nursing in the future. I felt uncomfortable uprooting Suba's flexible clinical position and also our children who were well settled in their early education at the nearby school. Both Suresh and Sunitha, who were now also well settled with their studies, had to be resettled again. The well-connected community that I was engaged in with my voluntary work, and my friends, were sad to hear of my decision to leave Brisbane.

With all the challenges ahead of us, the plan to move to Sydney had to be systematically managed as several of us would be affected if things went wrong. For the children, we were aware that there were several suitable public schools, including a secondary school for Sunitha, while Suresh could continue his studies at TAFE.

The schools that the children would attend had to be close enough to the rental property in Sydney so that they could walk every morning. I went on three occasions to Sydney to find a house to rent, but was unsuccessful.

Raj, my uncle's son who had helped me during my wedding, was returning to Malaysia after his engineering studies at Iowa University. He had accepted my suggestion to drop into Australia on his way home to explore the employment prospects just three weeks before our big move. He was also very surprised with my decision.

After a month of contemplation, I handed in my resignation letter to the hospital. The superintendent was concerned about my move to Sydney with six dependents under my care. I was confident that I would be able to find part-time work while studying my Masters full-time. At the

< 13 > Making my first brave move: Brisbane to Sydney

time, the vacancies for nursing positions were in high demand, which gave me the confidence that, somehow, we would manage the short-term financial crisis.

As planned, we agreed to leave the Brisbane house in a neat condition so that it was attractive to the rental market. We wanted the house to be rented quickly as we knew our cash-poor position and needed the money as soon as we got to Sydney. I had my last fortnight's salary and long service leave payment when I left the hospital, which was just enough to get a rental property for the first few weeks and no more. One month before the move, Suba and I had registered with the NSW Nurses Registration Board to obtain provisional certificates to work as RNs in NSW.

We were quite sad to leave our first family home that we had lived in for only six years. Like many other first-time owners, we had invested our feelings in the house as we furnished it, so it was natural that we were very emotional about leaving it for someone else to enjoy. As our first property and when we bought thinking that we would live in it forever. It did not occur to us that we might leave the place one day.

Meanwhile, I was glad to receive an offer for my Master of Nursing Administration course from the University of New South Wales, even though our accommodation in Sydney was still very uncertain. Apart from Raj and Suba, none of the others knew that at the end of the journey we had no accommodation in Sydney. I knew finding it was not going to be easy and hotels were beyond my budget. The only contingency plan I had was to check the vacancies at caravan parks that I had seen advertised in the local newspapers.

When I mentioned the possibility of staying in a caravan, the children were excited as they thought it would be a new and different experience, although it would not be as convenient as a house. Given the circumstances that we were in, there were no other choices, but to face and somehow, manage the challenging circumstances. We decided to stay in a caravan park accommodation when we reached Sydney.

As planned, three days before the departure all our household things were packed. Empty supermarket boxes of all sizes and old papers came in handy to carefully pack the breakable items. A few of the things we needed for daily use were left aside to be taken with us.

While we were caught up with the move and busy tidying the house, we decided to paint the house to freshen it up. I was aware that I had hay fever because of my allergies to pollen and house dust, but until then I did not realise that wet paint was equally problematic. As we were painting the house, I had a very irritating cough, which I thought could be due to my rising stress levels. By the time we finished painting the house, I was bedridden because the paint allergy had weakened me with general malaise, fever, joint pains, a headache and drowsiness. Fortunately, we had packed all the household things to put away in storage. My health was getting worse, but we were very fortunate to be invited to sleep over at a friend's place for a couple of nights to recover before the journey. As I was taken ill, Raj and Suresh ended up cleaning the last of the house rubbish. Luckily, the children did not feel the delay because they were kept busy with the swimming pool at a friend's place while I had some rest.

< 13 >   Making my first brave move: Brisbane to Sydney

After two days, I was regaining my strength and we started loading the car slowly and carefully. The night before the journey, Suresh's old *Holden Kingswood* and my small *Ford Laser* were all packed with our belongings. The anticipated departure time was delayed by four hours, but we finally left Brisbane at 10am. Although I was still feverish with a bad headache, I insisted on leaving without too much delay. Luckily, *Panadol kept* my headache under control as we began our journey, with Suresh, Anand and Raj in one car, and Sunitha, Anuja, Suba and myself in the second car.

The first day of the journey was exciting and a new experience for all of us, but we did not reach Sydney as planned. By the time we reached Coffs Harbour, it was getting dark and I was feeling the strain from driving as I was still recovering. We decided to stop around 7.30pm, but by then not many hotels were open nor had vacancies. I hadn't thought that the journey to Sydney would take us more than a day and therefore had no hotel reservation. Luckily, we managed to find accommodation that night in the only two rooms available in a motel.

It took an hour to unpack some of our personal things for sleeping. While Suba was busy with the children, I decided to jump into the pool to chill myself from the fever and to relax before going to bed. The next day, we set off after sunrise, and we knew that the journey would be quicker as we had completed two-thirds of it already.

Before I drove off from Coffs Harbour, I called our good family friend, Andrew. After my explanation, he insisted that I should drop in at his place, especially when he knew that I was not well and had not organised accommodation in Sydney. As we continued our journey, the fifth conversation with Andrew's mother was a serious insistence that I drop in with the family before checking into a caravan park. I thought of my tired family's welfare, especially the children who had been pretty good with the journey, and decided they definitely needed a comfortable bed and a good rest for the night. I had no choice but to drop in at Andrew's place.

The stopover turned into a sleepover for the seven of us that night. We were welcomed and they were glad to see us reach their home safely. That evening we had our showers in turn before we enjoyed the delicious, home-cooked dinner, which was different to Suba's cuisine. The sleep arrangement was a bit of a squeeze because of our large numbers, but, somehow, we all comfortably managed the night. Both Andrew and his mother were concerned for my health as they saw my tired look with a constant cough and high fever.

The next day, following the wonderful home-cooked Indian breakfast, I left the family behind and took a drive to Randwick, the suburb near the University of New South Wales (UNSW) to look for accommodation. Andrew's mother was very concerned with my health because she knew that I was ill and should rest, but I was more concerned with the members of my family who were dependent on me. Despite her warning, I left to search for a place in Randwick with Raj.

Both of us were surprised to note that all the real estate agencies were open and functioning in full swing on a Sunday. We did not waste any time, but quickly enquired after the available vacancies. We managed to see a few places around

< 13 > Making my first brave move: Brisbane to Sydney

the university that we thought would suit us, but by the time we returned to the agent's office we were told that the last few apartments were taken. I soon got the message that we might have to accept the available vacancies on the spot without delay to secure a place. I accepted a two-bedroom apartment on the third floor, which was not my preference. It had broken windows in the bedrooms, broken lamp shades in the hall, a small kitchen that could hardly fit more than one person at a time and was barely furnished, with old, shaky furniture. The rent for this apartment was $270, which I knew was far too high, but it was a supply/demand situation with Sydney rentals.

After completing the forms to accept the place, I had to pay a four weeks' rent in advance and four weeks' rent as the bond for the premises. When I paid with all the money I had, I was still $20 short, but Raj helped me out. I got the keys around 2.00pm that day and, feeling a bit more relaxed, I immediately went to fetch the family. After a late lunch at Andrew's place, we left for the new rental apartment.

The apartment was dull in appearance, but had some basic living items that we had to accept in our desperate situation. There was a dining room, two single beds in one room and a double bed in another room. There were no wardrobes or cupboards except for a pantry in the kitchen. Suba had looked forward to Sydney with excitement, but, upon the sight of the apartment, her enthusiasm disappeared at once. We consoled ourselves that it was going to be our interim home for the next twelve months until I completed my postgraduate studies. Meanwhile, we all cooperated and did our best with what we had. Anand and Anuja were excited with the large space as we walked in, but did not realise the household items would soon occupy most of it. On the other hand, Suresh was excited when he opened the balcony door to view the busy Botany Road below. It would keep him occupied with road gazing, unlike his bedroom in Brisbane that he found was too quiet for him.

Settling in busy Sydney was a big challenge for everyone in my family, especially in the first two weeks of getting there. Managing the first night at the Sydney apartment reminded me of my childhood in Malaysia, because there was hardly anything in the house, but we were safe together.

We all enjoyed bread, jam and cheese and some fresh fruit the first night at the apartment. We were aware that there was no television or other entertainment to keep the children occupied. To break the boredom, we all played a game of Monopoly which finished late into the night. The children were happy to stay up late because they were on holidays. Although we did not have that many clothes with us, we managed without too much discomfort because it was summer and the weather was comfortably warm. When everyone else had gone to sleep, Suba and I stayed up late planning how to find the earliest available nursing job. We knew we had only about $20 left in total if we closed all our bank accounts. I was also worried about finding my way in and around Sydney without getting lost.

The next morning, we left the apartment early in the morning to go to our scheduled appointments. We had the addresses of three nursing agencies with written directions

< 13 > Making my first brave move: Brisbane to Sydney

on how to get there before we started the journey. The first appointment was at a private agency. The appointment was only arranged for Suba, but I was invited in and allowed to sit with her while she was interviewed. Just before her interview finished, the manager asked me if I would be interested in working if a vacancy arose. Although we had planned for only Suba to work while I was still getting over my fever, because of our desperate financial situation I did not hesitate to accept the offer.

Before we left the agency, Suba had already agreed to work that night, whereas I had to wait until there was a vacancy. Although we had both agreed to work, I felt uncomfortable sending Suba to work on our first night in Sydney to manage our financial challenges. If I had a choice, I would rather see her stay at home with the children and look after me as I was feverish. We purchased some food and hurried home without delay so that Suba could have a rest before starting her ten-hour shift that evening.

I quickly managed to prepare a simple dinner by 5.00pm, and soon after we had a call from the same agency requesting me to work as well if I was available. While on the telephone, I looked at Suba for her approval, but Suba was more concerned about my health. We both knew the financial state we were in, so I returned the call agreeing to work on the same night, although I was still coughing and feverish. Soon the agency called back to confirm they had jobs for both of us at the same hospital. That night we were happy to leave the children at home with Raj and Suresh.

Suba and I had to leave the apartment well in time to find

our way to the assigned hospital. That night I was not in the mood to work as I was not feeling well at all. I was counting my hours to finish and Suba was exhausted when we drove home together. As soon as we reached the apartment, I got into the bed after a warm shower as I was still feverish and my health was getting worse. Following the children's breakfast, Suba brought mine with a couple of Panadols around 10.30am. She tried to sleep but found it hard.

After a couple of hours of rest, we both decided to go to the Prince of Wales Hospital (POWH), which was only a fifteen-minute walk from the apartment, to enquire about a permanent part-time position for Suba. Although we did not have an appointment, Suba managed to get an on-the-spot interview and was told that there were no vacancies for at least the next two weeks. In the interim, Suba had to cope with agency work and its erratic hours. Surprisingly, after three weeks Suba received a letter of employment at the POWH. We were happy with the offer because she got the Friday, Saturday and Sunday night shifts as requested, which was when I had no classes and could manage the children.

I also worked at night in the hospitals assigned by the agency. I found it very stressful to drive in Sydney, but could not forego work, given our poor financial position. Raj was also busy attending job interviews, but without much luck because he did not have local experience. He soon felt that he had tried enough places and decided to return to Malaysia. He was glad that he had the Sydney experience even though he did not get a job.

It did not take long for me to organise schools for Sunitha

< 13 > Making my first brave move: Brisbane to Sydney

and Anand. Sunitha was enrolled into Year 8 in a public school which was about fifteen minutes from the apartment, while Anand was enrolled in a kindergarten that was six hundred metres away. Suresh re-enrolled in his business studies at the local TAFE and managed the course himself. Closer to Anand's school, there was a preparatory class that Anuja was keen to attend after she spotted the children playing in the yard. We were lucky with the close proximity of the children's schools, all of which were within walking distance. Usually, I walked Anuja and Anand to their classes before I went to my university lectures. I realised that those moments were very challenging in my life, balancing my studies and working to cover my living expenses.

When the weekends came, the children were a bit restless because they were not kept busy and were often reminded to be quiet. I usually waited till Suba had a couple of hours of sound sleep after her night shift before I woke her to join us at the nearby beach. Sometimes on weekdays, I returned early from the library to take them to the beach at Coogee Bay, which was only a ten-minute drive. Anand and Anuja loved the cold, clean waters at the beach and got excited as they looked forward to playing in the shade, behind the rocks that safely blocked the high waves of the ocean. While they were enjoying the water, I managed to read my lecture notes while keeping an eye on them.

Before my semester one classes commenced, we had our first Christmas in Sydney. At that time, we did not know anyone in Sydney except Andrew and his family, and he invited us to his place on Christmas day. We met many of his friends and spent the day eating non-stop. My children were delighted to receive presents from us and Andrew's family, but we could not afford any gifts for the adults at their party. After the fun day, we left Andrew's place when it was close to midnight.

As the semester was approaching, I was a bit nervous about the studies ahead of me because I had not studied social science at a postgraduate level. The intensive course that I had enrolled in at UNSW was for one year (12 months) full-time, but those subjects such as accounting, law, health planning, health economics, were very unfamiliar to me and yet they were the generic compulsory subjects that were taught by relevant professional practitioners from various organisations.

The course commenced in late January with 60 postgraduate students from various disciplines. The course was interesting and challenging at the same time. On average, there was an assignment due each week. Several of the classes were held in the mornings, afternoons and evenings to suit many of the students who worked full-time. The expected allocated readings per week per subject took about three hours, which I found was difficult to spare with my part-time work and family commitments.

I knew my twelve months in Sydney was going to be very stressful; therefore, I wanted to ensure that I maintained my physical fitness. It did not take me long to locate the university sports facilities that were easily accessible from my residence. I often took everyone from home with me to exercise at the available indoor sports at the games halls. Badminton was the

< 13 > Making my first brave move: Brisbane to Sydney

game that all four children, Suba and I most enjoyed. We often spent no less than two hours playing, at a time.

Apart from the sports and games amenities, I made certain that I knew where the nearest library facilities were and quickly learned how to access the available services. I found the seats in the library more comfortable than my own dining table. The library lighting was far brighter and suitable for night reading than the low watt lightbulbs I had in the apartment. During my assignment submission times, I very much looked forward to spending my productive study hours in the library and often found it difficult to leave.

Although lectures had begun, I still continued shift work at the private nursing homes to earn some cash. I commenced work at two nursing homes during the first week of the first semester. On days when I had morning classes, I managed to work in the afternoon and even on nights at the nearby nursing homes. If the classes were in the afternoon the next day, I squeezed in a shift in the morning as I was very tight for cash.

I had to let go of the extra shifts after a few weeks of the course as I had extensions for my weekly assignments. Sometimes, I was only physically present at the lectures while my brain was too tired to concentrate because I mentally drained from shift work. Suba had warned me that I was too exhausted, both physically and mentally, to keep up with my post-graduate study commitments. I realised I had to trim down my work hours to catch up with my lost time for studies, otherwise resigning from my previous job to gain my postgraduate qualification would have been a waste.

I gradually came to know many of my peers, who were studying full-time with full scholarships, were enjoying the course and the social meetings, which I often missed out on. If I had been as financially fortunate as my peers, I would have loved to attend all the group meetings that were extremely valuable for group assignments. They often had time to discuss the key points at group meetings as well to complete the required readings before they completed the assignments.

Even though I missed out on some opportunities, I cherished keeping my family together despite our limited luxuries. Despite our poor financial position, we were still happy to be living together as a family in the crowded apartment. There were many great moments, with occasional outbursts, mainly between Suresh and Sunitha. At times, the children had several warnings not to jump on the floor as there were people living below us. The morning scenes were unforgettable with the usual rush for the use of the single toilet and bathroom for all six of us. The morning commotion could start if Suresh got into the bathroom before others because he often took well over ten minutes. Sometimes, Sunitha and Anuja shared their showers, which helped to reduce the waiting time for others. Knowing the poor shower facility at the apartment, Suba often had her wash at the hospital before she returned from work. I escaped the queue as I was up earlier than the rest in the family, so I had the bathroom all to myself without anyone yelling at me to hurry up. On occasion, I had my shower at the university sport facilities after class.

Despite the numerous family and work challenges I faced, I still managed to pass my subjects successfully. It was a big

< 13 > Making my first brave move: Brisbane to Sydney

relief when I finally graduated with my Master of Nursing Administration, while keeping my family intact.

The one Sydney experience that remained with us, apart from my postgraduate graduation, was one that happened to my son just before I completed my studies. On his last day of prep, when my wife and I attended the parent-teacher meeting, we were told by the relief teacher of Anand's unfair treatment at the school. The relief teacher disclosed to us that Anand had been isolated from the class group activities as a punishment by his regular teacher, who had gone on maternity leave. Unfortunately, we heard this news on the last day of Anand's school, so we did not have the opportunity to talk to any school staff and could not take the issue any further. We were very disheartened with the experience of racism that Anand had to go through at that very young age.

On the other hand, Anuja, who was nearly three years old, had no issues with her kindergarten sessions, where many of the children were from Eastern European background. She loved attending the kindergarten three days a week and thoroughly enjoyed the company of her teachers and classmates, who often came up to chat when we took Anuja there.

I felt very valued when a senior position as Assistant Director in Human Resources at the Royal North Shore Hospital was offered after an elective placement. I discussed the offer with Suba and decided not to accept because my two young children's needs were more important than my career. The twelve months of my study posed a big challenge not only for me, but also for the family who lived in cramped conditions because of my career decision and I was thankful to my wife and children for putting up with it for my career. I had decided that I would not subject them to the same situation, not even for one day, after my course.

I was deprived of paternal love when I was growing up, and I remembered how much I missed my dad and did not want a similar situation for my children, especially in their formative years. The Sydney experience was different to Brisbane, with some great moments of joy. We had made several new friends in the short time of twelve months. The long-term plan for Suba and me was to move away from busy Sydney to a quieter place with opportunities for the children's education with a lower cost of living. We searched for vacancies in the national newspapers in regional and rural Australia.

I came across a vacancy for a teaching position just as I was about to finish my course. After I submitted my application to the Ballarat College of Advanced Education (BCAE), I wanted to know more about the location and college. After further reading and talking to some of my postgraduate classmates about Ballarat, who had very positive remarks about the place, we decided to take the plunge and see what awaited us. When the children heard of our plan to move again, they were excited. They felt that the next interstate journey would be equally as exciting as the last one. They were looking forward with anticipation while Suba and I waited for an employment offer.

Within a week I was shortlisted and had to skip my classes to attend the interview, so I did not have the time to look around Ballarat or the BCAE when I went. The very fact that

< 13 > Making my first brave move: Brisbane to Sydney

it was quieter and greener grabbed my interest instantly. I was very fortunate to receive an offer as a Lecturer in Nursing.

Suba was happy that there was a position waiting for me as soon as I finished the course. She knew that our circumstances would change for the better when I started working rather than depending on part-time wages. We both felt a sense of relief and hoped that the hassles we faced would come to an end when we left Sydney. I wanted our children, who had been supportive of my career aspirations, to experience much better living conditions. I was dreaming and counting the days before we left Sydney and started earning some money to provide Suba some relief! By the time our twelve months in Sydney was coming to an end, I could see family burdens and work stress getting to Suba as well. She too felt the children, who had been living in sub-standard accommodation and under stressful circumstances, needed a change.

‹ **14** ›

Embracing the second move:
Sydney to Ballarat

Once again, we had to prepare ourselves for the move. Having had our Brisbane to Sydney experience, we were more aware of the work involved for the second relocation. Luckily, we did not have to pack all our things because some of them were still packed from the previous move. I was less anxious about this move because I knew I had a job waiting for me. When we reached Ballarat (in Victoria), I would immediately have an income, and we were confident that Suba would find a position without delay, given her experience and qualifications.

The children's excitement was building and mine was as well; we were looking forward to the journey at the end of the year and I could not wait to hand in my last assignment. The children welcomed the idea that the journey would take more than two days and we would treat the trip as a travelling mini-holiday.

Meanwhile, we heard that Suba's brother, Faisal, planned

to visit us with his family. When we heard of their intended visit, we were excited, but at the same time our tight financial position would be strained hosting them. The twelve months of survival in Sydney with Suba's wages and my limited income only covered the essentials and we did not have any cash saved. The only way we could manage the journey to Ballarat was to use our credit cards. I knew that was not a sound decision, but it was the only choice we had.

Suba was most definitely geared up and looking forward to a break as she had been the worker and child-minder for twelve months. I had become sick of study and was physically exhausted from part-time shift work during my free time. The stress from demanding, compulsory lectures, examination preparations and assignment submissions, definitely burned me out. Meanwhile, the children, who had only minimal attention from me, were equally waiting for when I would be spending quality time with them, so we were all looking forward to the journey.

At that time, Raj had already left for Malaysia and Suresh and Sunitha were still with us. We knew that Anand, Anuja and Sunitha had to follow us to continue their schooling, whereas Suresh still had to finish his certificate course. He was not happy to be left behind in Sydney, but Suba advised him that completing his TAFE course in Sydney was his highest priority. Although he was twenty-one at the time, he still lacked self-confidence and had to seek advice from Suba for everything he did. We were not happy to leave him behind, but encouraged him to live by himself for a month before we left for Ballarat.

Sunitha was studying Year 10 and had no choice but to follow us. We could not leave her alone as she was too young and had no one to support and guide her.

By the time Faisal, Arnie and their two daughters joined us in Sydney, we had organised our household things to be delivered to Ballarat through a removalist. The two cars (one hired) for the two families of nine people in total, left Sydney as planned. We stopped at a few places on the way to relax and sightsee as the children requested. Finally, we reached our destination after five days on the road. The BCAE (later known as Federation University) had organised an apartment along the Western Freeway (10km outside of Ballarat) as our temporary accommodation until we found a permanent place to rent.

The reserved apartment had ample space for all nine of us to sleep. Outside, there was a large space that was safe for the children to run around to keep themselves busy. The spacious room had comfortable bunk beds for each of us with a fully-furnished kitchen that was handy for cooking our own meals. During the time we were there, we did not see any other guests at the apartments, so we had the whole place to ourselves.

The two weeks of privacy was quite exciting for the children as they treated the place as their own and were busy playing outside in the fine summer weather. Sunitha usually ended up as their babysitter, although they did not need her. Suba and her sister-in-law, Arnie, had a lot to catch up on about their families in Malaysia, so they were busy chatting all the time. Faisal relaxed and enjoyed the fresh, sunny air of Ballarat while sipping some of the locally produced wines.

< 14 >   Embracing the second move: Sydney to Ballarat

The next morning after arriving in Ballarat, I reported to the Head of Nursing, who was very pleased to see me and offered her assistance to get me quickly settled into Ballarat's regional lifestyle. I admired her caring nature and demeanour that made me feel very welcome. Her inquiry about my family's wellness and keenness to meet them indicated to me that she also cared for her staff and their family's health.

Once we arrived in Ballarat, Suba and I checked daily for a suitable house to rent. We followed up with all of the real estate agents for a rental property. Although it was time-consuming, it had to be done because the university had only provided two weeks' accommodation, with the expectation that we would find a home in that time. The rental properties in Ballarat at that time (1988) were much cheaper compared to Sydney, so we felt it was manageable.

After few days of exhaustive searching, we decided to rent an old three-bedroom brick- veneer house within our price range. Suba and I thought that it was not the best choice, but it was much better than the Sydney apartment. Within a week, we moved into the house, located in Wendouree (a Ballarat suburb) that was not far from the magnificent Lake Wendouree.

For all of us, Ballarat was very beautiful with its lake, gardens, trees and hills. Suba and I wanted to absorb the natural beauty of Ballarat over time and did not want to rush and visit everything within a few days, but we followed Faisal and his family as they had limited time here.

They recalled the scenic trees and mountains they saw when they drove along the highway from Melbourne to

Ballarat. They were equally excited upon seeing Ballarat's other beauties. Without a doubt, Lake Wendouree and the beautiful botanical gardens with its swings became the children's most favourite place. As a group, we also experienced the mineral water at Daylesford Central Springs (60km from Ballarat) and rowing a boat on Lake Daylesford. Suba and I felt that Ballarat was like a holiday destination, with so many beautiful places to discover.

When the two weeks of Faisal's family's companionship ended, we were all sad to see them leave, but it was harder for the children as they'd had such a wonderful time together in the new place. Faisal and Arnie had also had a good break as the children were having fun with their similar-age cousins.

As soon as Faisal and family left Ballarat, our settlement planning began. Firstly, I organised Anand into a public school before the school semester commenced. We found we were zoned for Wendouree Primary School, and that Anuja had to wait another year before she was eligible to go to kindergarten. Sunitha was enrolled into Year 11 at the nearest secondary school only eight hundred metres from the house.

Sunitha still needed assistance with her schoolwork because of the adjustments she had made over the last few years: from the death of Suba's mother, to new guardians and moving to a new country with strangers. When she joined us in Brisbane, we found her confidence and self-esteem were very poor. I knew that settling into her third Australian school within four years must have been difficult for her, so whenever I had free time, I helped her with her schoolwork. I often spent time with her on the weekends when the other children were in bed and Suba was at work. Initially, she was hesitant to ask for help, but she became more communicative and thus made progress.

Once we had organised schools for Sunitha and Anand, Suba was lucky to find employment on Friday, Saturday and Sunday nights at the local Base Hospital. On those days, I was with the children while she was at work.

The rented house in Wendouree was close to all amenities. It was convenient for shopping, playgrounds, schools and Suba's work, except it was about 15km from my work. Suba was still not confident to drive the car by herself despite the light traffic in Ballarat, so I had the car to drop Sunitha and Anand from their schools on my way to work and to fetch them home. Some days I returned to office after bringing them home as we were not in any position to purchase a second car.

Some days when I came home early from work, I took the three children to the park where they enjoyed a few minutes of exercise to refresh themselves after their full day at school. On weekends, Suba came along to the parks after she'd had some sleep following her night shift. On the very few days when Suba did not work on the weekends, all of us visited new places around Ballarat.

The following year, when Anuja turned three-and-a-half years, she could not wait to be enrolled in kindergarten three days a week. She was happy to leave us to join her classmates each morning, which was quite emotional for us.

Within a couple of months, we found the rented house had dampness in all the rooms. The advancing dampness aggravated Sunitha's asthma, which flared up quite regularly.

Luckily, we somehow, managed the asthma episodes without hospitalisation. Anuja also had a few asthmatic attacks, and Suba and I often fell ill in that house. The regular illness made us decide to search for a better house within our budget, either to rent or purchase.

Although I had five years of experience teaching nursing, I still was nervous when I started my position at the BCAE School of Nursing. All the staff welcomed me and I was able to answer their questions about my qualifications, work experience and cultural background. At the time, none of the academic staff at the school had postgraduate qualifications except for certificates from the hospitals, which was adequate to teach the students in the Diploma course. In those years, nursing was a new tertiary discipline, so it was not surprising that my boss, the Head of School, had only a Bachelor's degree.

I found my Bachelor of Science with Honours was more applicable at the university level than at the Princess Alexandra Hospital. I was able to teach the sciences much more in-depth to tertiary students who were able to grasp the concepts more readily than the hospital-trained nursing students. My simplistic, dot point lecture notes linked clearly with the learning outcome objectives of the subjects and were greatly appreciated, particularly by those who had not done sciences at secondary school.

My students enjoyed the way I taught them because I had very clear lesson objectives and I often quizzed them on previous lessons before starting the new concepts for the day. Students found the quiz was very nerve-racking, but they welcomed it because it was informal ongoing revision.

My students never missed my lectures. There was always 100 percent attendance, despite me telling them that I would not penalise them for absences. The regular high feedback score (4.5/5) from them motivated me to maintain my teaching quality. Their positive remarks about how my lectures were meaningful to them, easy to follow, fun and engaging and also, indicated how much they valued them. They equally enjoyed the guest speakers I carefully selected from relevant organisations.

My relationship with the students had always been professionally excellent. Many of them did not hesitate to drop in to see me or just to say, 'Hello' as they passed my office. They respected me for treating them as adults and not treating them as less important.

When I commenced delivering the second-year subjects, the third-year curriculum was being developed concurrently and I was involved in developing and delivering some of the third-year units. Not long after, the Diploma course was upgraded to a Bachelor's degree, followed by several other postgraduate courses. The school continued its expansion further to deliver the program in Hong Kong. As the enrolment of international students in the undergraduate and postgraduate nursing courses expanded, the number of academic staff increased.

My appointment at the school began as a lecturer and soon expanded to include other roles as assigned by the Head of School. Over the years, I held several posts including Course Coordinator for Graduate Diploma, Selection Officer, Clinical Coordinator for Undergraduate Program, etc.

Apart from the roles I held within the school, I also served on several university committees. Student Loans Committee, University Academic Board, University Research Committee, President of the Staff Social club, and Staff Association, among others.

I also enjoyed the annual university events, such as the Graduation days and Open Days. With further growth of the university, several name changes took place for the BCAE. Firstly, it was the Ballarat University College, then it became The University of Ballarat. It is currently known as Federation University Australia.

One major benefit with the university position was its flexibility, which was a great advantage for me at the time as I could fetch the children from their schools.

Suba felt that Ballarat had excellent opportunities for her to pursue a postgraduate course. She thought that a course in Health Education would be relevant and appropriate following her Health Visitor course from UK. After we discussed how we would manage our challenges across work, study and family commitments, Suba commenced the Graduate Diploma in Health Education at BCAE with a scholarship that covered her tuition fees.

As the course began, Suba was occupied to the maximum. She had to care for the children and worked as an RN at the Ballarat Base Hospital on weekends, while two evenings a week she attended classes. Suba managed to take Anuja to kindergarten on a bicycle in the mornings, which allowed me to use the car. Anuja, who thoroughly enjoyed her kindergarten social life often made us wait as she farewelled her friends with

< 14 > Embracing the second move: Sydney to Ballarat

kisses before getting into the car. Anand and Sunitha often waited at a regular pick-up spot for me. As soon as I got home, I assisted Suba with the remaining chores, and some days I had to return to office to complete my unfinished work.

On the days Suba had classes, I ensured I was home early to look after the children while Suba prepared herself for BCAE. I often prepared dinner for the family, showered them, discussed their school activities and listened to their school stories before they fell asleep.

By the time Suba returned from her evening class, the house was quiet as the children were sleeping. We capitalised on those moments to discuss Suba's assignments and course progress.

With our busy lifestyles, the two years of her part-time studies went by very swiftly. Her grades were at distinction level and above, which maintained her scholarship. At the end of two years, Suba successfully completed her course and graduated with a Graduate Diploma in Health Education.

Five years after I had joined BCAE, I explored pursuing my doctoral studies with Melbourne University. Although the University of Melbourne had no nursing faculties at that time, it had a very good international reputation for successful completion of PhDs. After my preliminary discussion with the Head of Program Evaluation at the University of Melbourne, Dr Gerald Elsworth, he was satisfied with my qualifications and encouraged me to submit my formal enrolment for PhD candidature. He knew the research process and protocols very well as he had an outstanding track record of PhD supervision.

The first six months of my regular face-to-face meetings

with Gerald to discuss my research topic were very useful, and at the same time I had doubts whether I was a suitable candidate. After reading several journal articles on evaluation, my initially vague idea of the research topic became clearer. My ongoing discussions with Gerald, who guided my research pathway systematically, enabled me to finally submit my research proposal with confidence.

I was also lucky to get a PhD Higher Education Contribution Studies (HECS) scholarship which exempted me from my tuition fees. The HECS scholarship assisted my study without any interruption to my ongoing monthly financial commitments.

Soon after enrolment, I established a routine to drive the ninety-minute journey to Melbourne University to meet up with my supervisor. Gerald always read my corrected work and looked forward to our two-hour meetings in his office to provide feedback. Sometimes the in-depth discussion went well over three hours. Gerald's valued critical remarks and professional guidance was well beyond my expectations.

His encouragement of me to actively participate in the fortnightly mandatory school evaluation seminars on a diverse range of innovative approaches to evaluation was also very valuable for my PhD progress.

The long and hard six-year journey finally ended when I handed in my thesis for assessment. I could not believe it was accepted with a complete pass without any changes or amendments! The new Head of Program Evaluation personally commended me for such an outstanding achievement!

< 14 > Embracing the second move: Sydney to Ballarat

It would have been a greater moment if I had my parents to hear those remarkable comments or witness my graduation. I wondered how happy they would have been to see me receiving the highest qualification, but my great day was shared with my wife and my two children. I would not have completed my studies without their support and patience. I was happy to reach that highest level, which I had never dreamt of until I joined the university sector. To me it was a great day in my life to know I had done it!

While I was in the middle of my doctoral studies, Suba was enjoying her teaching position at the Queen Elizabeth Centre (QEC, later part of Ballarat Health Services) and decided that she would continue her career permanently in education. When we initially discussed her pursuing postgraduate studies after her Graduate Diploma of Health Education, she dismissed moving into education. She was unsure of the academic challenges and her stamina. Her full-time work as a Nurse Educator at the QEC was already demanding.

One of her other concerns was that her study might cut into her teaching preparation time and lower her performance at work. She did not want to lower her outstanding feedback from students that kept her highly motivated. It was only after further discussion that she agreed to embark on the four-year, part-time course. Meanwhile her application for a scholarship was also successful.

Finally, she enrolled herself in a Master of Education (Administration and Curriculum Development) at the School of Education at the University of Ballarat. We knew that we were going to be very busy with our studies and full-time work, so we both agreed to help each other where possible to manage the house and the children.

Just about the time Suba was embarking on her postgraduate studies Sunitha, who had turned eighteen, decided to move out of the house to live independently. She took a part-time job at a fast food outlet to have a break from her studies; we had encouraged her to do whatever she wanted, but promised to help her if needed. Everyone missed her, but we kept the children busy to distract them.

My weekends would start early in the garden, weeding and pruning. The children promised to help and would join me after their breakfast, but they found it difficult to stay for long. They enjoyed the brief outdoor learning sessions in the garden about the animals they came across including snails, slugs, earthworms and woodlice. Again, the learning session could not captivate them for long, but I was able to answer their inquisitive questions at a level they could understand.

Usually, by 11:30am we would end up shopping and return with the week's groceries that the children would love to help me to put away in the pantry. They would also volunteer to help me with the cooking, which was more of a hassle than help, but I let them anyway. By the time we finished our lunch, Anand and Anuja would have organised the games to follow lunch. Their chosen card games, quizzes or movies often extended well into early evening. If Suba had weekend classes, I preferred to spend the quality time with the children in the beautiful parks and gardens around the lake. Once we reached home, they again would volunteer to assist me in preparing dinner before Suba returned.

We noticed an interesting pattern in the children's study. They began to bring their books to the same table we studied at to finish their given homework or school projects without any prompts. They were motivated when they saw us spending time on our books at home.

Suba found the course was much more worthwhile than she anticipated. One of the best outcomes was from her minor thesis that focused on improving nurse recruitment into aged care settings.

As most of her peers were also working full-time with family commitments, a high attrition rate for the course was inevitable, but, fortunately, Suba stayed in the course and managed to receive very high grades for her assignments. She was glad to be one of four students to complete the course successfully after four years of study. The children and I were equally glad to see her graduate.

The life in Ballarat was busy with study and work, for both Suba and I, but we still enjoyed our moments with the children and Sunitha.

I remember that I was completely exhausted before the second semester ended. Those were the times when grades for the assignments and examination papers had to be collated and marked, to be released before students went on their summer holidays. I often looked forward to the semester break just like university students to re-energise me before the new semester commenced. I appreciated those breaks as they coincided with Victorian school holidays.

One of the memorable moments during the holidays was our annual trip to Brisbane. We all enjoyed the trips so much that it became an annual event while the children were still in school. We all loved visiting Brisbane because we had lived there for five years and Anuja was born there. Although we had left Brisbane and moved to Sydney for a year and ended up in Ballarat, the children had maintained contact with their childhood friends. For Suba and me, Brisbane was the first place we had lived in Australia. We had fond memories of our first home and the quality time we spent with our children. More interestingly, our family friends, Gana and Angie, still lived there while we had moved around. They missed us and loved the children dearly. They also often looked forward for our annual visit.

In those days we could not afford to fly, so we, somehow, had to manage the twenty-four-hour journey in our manual hatchback *Ford Laser*.

The children had books, cards, board games, writing pads and other gadgets to keep them occupied during travel. All of us enjoyed the stops every three to four hours for toilet breaks or simply to run around in the parks to break the monotonous journey and to refresh ourselves. The children knew that I had to stop the vehicle if they needed a toilet break, but often ended up in them getting icy poles as well.

One of the challenging situations during the trip was travelling in a car with no air-conditioning in summer when the temperature was above 36°C. Our innovative idea was to place wet towels on the closed window screens and a wet handkerchief over the car ventilation outlet, which managed to cool the car as we travelled. We wore light clothes and constantly cooled ourselves with the water that we carried.

We maintained our fluid intake and had ample homemade, lemon ice cubes to suck on to quench our thirst and make the journey manageable. My favourite stops were the free showers at roadside cafes along the highway to freshen up while the others were having a hot drink.

The conversations we had in the car while travelling were valuable to Suba and me as parents as we shared our thoughts with the children. The atmosphere and the holiday mood in the car allowed the children to freely express their thoughts about their school and to talk about their ambitions. They knew very little about us as their parents, so it was not a surprise when asked about our past. Without hesitation, we shared our childhood days in Malaysia and how we met and continued our studies while they were born. We welcomed their views on how Suba and I could be better parents for them. The conversation also included the sharing of housework. We felt great listening to their well-conceptualised views of the world and family at that young age. Overall, the long journey was not just a holiday time, but also offered a moment for valuable family discussions and reflections.

By the end of the twenty-four-hour journey, we wanted to get out of the car as we were already looking forward to Gana and Angie's warm hospitality.

‹ 15 ›

Applying the synergy of community engagements and my career path

I have always pursued my passion for community work at local, state and national levels. My community engagement that began at the local scene slowly crept into international level.

When I was appointed as a lecturer in 1988 at the School of Nursing, I saw a need to establish a centre to support the City of Ballarat's culturally diverse individuals and communities. According to Victorian history, the people of Chinese origin who worked in the gold mines in the 1850s had all left as there was very poor support and no appreciation of Chinese cultural heritage. In 1988, there were only a few Chinese residents and nearly all of them owned their own businesses to support themselves, as finding employment was hard unless they were one of the few who managed to find work with the government. At that time, Ballarat's population was 83000 and over 98 percent were from Anglo-Saxon backgrounds.

A small group of people from culturally and linguistically

diverse backgrounds (CALD), mainly South Asian, raised the idea for a place for them to meet and celebrate cultural festivals. As an active member of that group, I was keen to support their unmet needs.

A small committee was soon formed and, as the elected president, I handled most of the secretarial work and agenda items for the small, dedicated group. The initial membership of fifteen soon grew beyond eighty and thus the BAAA (Ballarat Asian-Australian Association) was established. Several of the well-attended functions were hosted at the Ballarat College for Advanced Education (BCAE) with Asian dinners and featured some dedicated local performers.

The excellent publicity of BAAA events, through the local paper, leaflets and flyers, expanded to attract more than one hundred and sixty people as regular patrons. Following these successful events, the executive committee discussed how to embrace the community more widely to include people from the Central Highlands region, which led to the formation of the Central Highlands Asian-Australian Association of Victoria Incorporated (CHAAAVI).

Once the community understood the objectives of CHAAAVI, they did not hesitate to continue their full support, including the local notaries. With the continued funding support from state and local government, the valued community engagements kept on expanding. As the fully committed interim president, I never declined any invitations to speak at public functions to promote the organisation.

At the time in Ballarat, there were several other ethno-specific organisations that held their own activities. None of these organisations was large enough to host one main event to embrace all ethno-specific cultures under one umbrella, so there was a need for those smaller organisations to unite to form a stronger and larger body in order to have a stronger voice on behalf of all CALD groups in the region which will help them to successfully attract funds from government bodies.

The City of Ballarat supported and facilitated the groups creating a single organisation that would advocate on behalf of all ethno-specific groups. At the time, there were several ethno-specific organisations, but not united under one umbrella, so there were no strong voices on CALD concerns. A scheduled meeting was called to debate numerous practical issues, as well as the new organisation's name. The new organisation was publicly accepted by all the community groups in and around Ballarat, as the Ballarat Regional Multicultural Council (BRMC).

The Ballarat local government, the individual ethno-specific clubs and other groups in the region, the Ethnic Communities' Council of Victoria (the main Victoria organisation for CALD communities) and the Victorian Multicultural Commission (VMC) endorsed the establishment of the BRMC and offered their support for its development as the key body in the Central Highlands region. As the interim elected chairperson, I was instrumental in liaising with key organisations in the region to form strong ongoing partnerships and secure financial assistance for the BRMC.

Local government appreciated the community need for

the BRMC, so we were invited to several cultural advisory discussions. I remember one day I had a call at work from the Mayor's office requesting a lunch meeting with the Mayor. The meeting was to advise the Mayor on the local government strategy framework of how to support and manage concerns about the growing numbers of CALD migrant population who wanted to settle in Ballarat.

On another occasion, I instituted a practical resolution strategy for cultural conflict at the workplace following the hospital CEO's invitation. The implementation of the strategy effectively reduced workplace conflicts and markedly improved the working collaboration of health professionals, thus improving the productivity of the hospital.

My vision to establish the BRMC for the community not only produced tangible benefits for the community, but also lifted my profile. As time progressed, my cultural interests and community engagement expanded into the state level.

In the years that followed, not only did I deliver talks at various local clubs, such as Rotary, Lions and Men's Group, but was also invited to join the executive board of the Ethnic Communities' Council of Victoria (ECCV), improving the profile of the BRMC. At the time, Mr George Lekakis, the Chairperson of the ECCV, saw the need to make the regional communities as part of the ECCV organisation. Later, George nominated me as the Regional Representative for ECCV. At the full Board meetings, I was given the opportunity to raise the issues that concerned CALD communities in rural and regional Victoria.

My continued role as an advocate for rural communities

saw me invited on several state-level advisory boards, including Human Services, the Victorian Rural Human Services Strategy Project Advisory Board to the Minister for Health, and the Victorian Ministerial Advisory Council on Cultural and Linguistic Diversity. My passionate advocacy roles at the state level soon progressed to the national arena. Over time, I served as the nominated regional representative for ECCV, but, after a couple of years, I was nominated to stand for election at the national level by the ECCV. I was elected as the Regional Chairperson to represent all regional ethnic communities' councils in Australia. After serving my two year-term as the Regional Chairperson for Federation of the Ethnic Communities' Councils of Australia (FECCA), I was again asked to consider to be nominated as a Deputy Chairperson for FECCA. Again, I was successfully elected as one of the two Senior Deputy Chairperson of FECCA. Although FECCA was an NGO (non-government organisation), the issues tabled by FECCA were often a "face-to-face" dialogue with ministers and Opposition Party leaders who gave serious considerations to CALD concerns. The Federal Government was the key funding organisation for FECCA as it represented the issues that relate to CALD communities in Australia.

My passion for cultural interests was not limited to Australia, but, amazingly, opened the doors for international links.

One of the valuable engagements I completed internationally was developing the health services management program for Indonesian senior health professionals in medicine, dentistry, pharmacy, nursing and hospital administration.

My expertise in curriculum development, ability to communicate in Bahasa and also my knowledge of the Muslim culture (as an ex-Malaysian) served me well as a consultant for AusAid. Apart from enriching my cultural knowledge, I witnessed the huge gaps between the rich and poor living conditions in Indonesia. Witnessing young children begging on the streets for food brought back memories of my own poverty in Malaysia. Although I had hardly anything to eat at home in my young days, I did not beg.

During the delivery of my lectures in Indonesia, the extreme courtesy and hospitality of staff during our presence in the Sulawesi World Health Organisation centre to deliver the program was praiseworthy and always made me want me to revisit the country.

One other international opportunity in cultural diversity was my visit to Japan. It would not have happened if I did not encounter Ms Michiko, a politically-well-connected, wealthy entrepreneur who visited Ballarat Nursing Homes regularly from Japan.

I happened to meet her at a dinner organised by the hospital, when she invited me to visit her hospital in Japan. My basic communication in Japanese that I had learned at the Victorian School of Languages must have impressed her, together with my professional credentials. I confessed to her that my interest in language was triggered by Suba (my wife), who was the one who wanted to improve her communication with Japanese visitors in the first place.

Ms Michiko mentioned that my basic Japanese reading, writing and speaking skills were sufficient to engage with the health professionals in Japan and to advance further with the language. She also anticipated that I would share my health expertise with Japanese health professionals. Knowing my financial situation, she invited me to spend three weeks in Japan and agreed to fully support my food, lodging and local travel expenses. After discussing it with Suba, we both felt her kind offer was too good to miss.

I was excited for the opportunity, but was still very nervous of the cultural challenges I would face. Going to a country for the first time, even if you can speak their language, is still very challenging. I had a challenging time with English when I first arrived in the UK, even after years of practice. Therefore, the Japanese language, which I had learned only for a year, could definitely impose a greater challenge when I got there.

Ms Michiko was amazed that I managed the three-hour train journey by myself after landing in Tokyo, before being fetched by her hospital staff. After an impressive hospital tour, I shared my experiences with the senior staff and board members of the hospital to answer their questions on health-related issues. That evening at the grand surprise reception at the hospital, my command of the Japanese language was certainly tested to its limits. As the chief guest, I had to introduce myself in Japanese. The remaining days in Japan had a full itinerary every day from early morning until 11.00pm, which exhausted me. Somehow, I managed them without missing any, as the Japanese are very strict about punctuality and appointments. My cultural interest and sharing of my health expertise established a trusting relationship, and it did not surprise me when I was invited for two further visits to Japan under their full sponsorship.

One of the main advantages of community engagement was the opportunity to develop my leadership skills, the lack of which had limited my academic career path. Fortunately, I was able to demonstrate the leadership skills I acquired doing voluntary work, which were equally valuable and transferable to formal work settings.

I had enjoyed my academic career with the University of Ballarat since I joined the organisation in 1988, but the opportunities for senior positions or career advancement was very limited. I decided to leave the University of Ballarat in 2006 after eighteen years' service, which was partly related to being overloaded with work.

Not long after, I was offered a Senior Lecturer position from the University of Melbourne's Rural Clinical School at Shepparton to direct the Rural Health Module to highlight the health needs of rural and regional communities. After my discussion with Suba and my children, I accepted the full-time position, which was 300km away from Ballarat. My community engagement with FECCA continued and I was elected again as the Deputy Chairperson.

At that time, Anand (my son) had graduated from his combined degree in Systems Engineering and Computer Science and was working in Nuremburg in Germany. Anuja (my daughter) was completing her double degrees in Business (Accounting) and Banking and Finance, while Suba continued her full-time work with Ballarat Health Services.

I had to reside in Shepparton as it was not practical to travel the 300km to work each day. After six months of free accommodation at the University residence, with the family's approval I purchased a comfortable house in Shepparton closer to the campus.

Shepparton became a family gathering place as it comfortably accommodated all my family and their friends in its four large bedrooms. My daughter came down with Suba to spend her free days in Shepparton during her course. My son visited with his friends from Nuremburg during the Christmas break. Suba came at least once a month and, in return, I went to Ballarat between her visits. We also spent time together in Ballarat during my clinical site visits to the Grampians region.

The new position gave me total academic freedom over the compulsory four-week Rural Health Unit (RHU) component for final year University of Melbourne medical students. The changes I introduced improved the outcome of the course and enticed the medical students to return to practice in rural Australia on finishing their medical degrees. Thus, my work contributed very successfully to help to address the shortage of doctors in regional and rural areas.

The excellent comments from the Head of the School not only boosted my leadership role, but also increased my salary by 40 percent. The enjoyable work at the rural campus and professional peer support motivated me to expand my untapped leadership skills even further.

It was timely when I explored the next obvious level of progression in my career, the professorship level, which I secured at the School of Medicine and Dentistry at James Cook University (JCU) in Townsville, Queensland.

The professorial appointment at JCU Medical School was quite different to my previous position in Shepparton, where I had focused on the rural health component of the course in the final year of a six-year program. In Townsville, I taught the first- and second-year cohorts of 200 students in the undergraduate medical program. I also mentored the students and supported their welfare needs.

I helped the school in developing new postgraduate courses while enjoying the company of the teaching team from medicine, nursing, veterinary science, pharmacy, physiotherapy and education. My community engagement leadership skills at the professorial level were appreciated by the local diverse communities in Townsville, including the indigenous communities, where I was fully engaged, after work-hours.

The thought of leaving the position was not easy because I had overcome numerous hurdles and moments of despair on my way to achieve it, but my family was my highest priority. I reflected on how I missed my dad from an early age and often wished he was alive. Likewise, I felt the need to be around my children and wife as they are the most precious things I will ever have. I did not want them to miss me as I had missed my parents.

Townsville's northern Queensland location meant high humidity and a regular monsoon rainfall that made it difficult for me to drive on the flooded roads. It was a popular holiday city on a beautiful coastline, but was an expensive place to rent in.

The four-hour flight from Townsville to visit Suba, the tropical weather and my loneliness made me finally to resign my Associate Professor position at JCU. Following the academic farewell party from the school and two other farewells from the community groups, I left Townsville in good spirit. I was glad to be back in Ballarat and with Suba and my two children, who were very pleased with my return. Apart from my wife and children, the local Ballarat community were equally happy to see me back. The cooler weather and the warm reception of familiar faces gave me a feeling of connectedness to my old community that I had known since 1988.

The university senior positions that I held also profiled with further leadership skills that would be equally relevant for positions in the NGOs in the community. The ECCV, under the leadership of Mr Eddie Mcliffe, quickly co-opted me back onto the Board. The new position on the ECCV Board allowed me to strengthen the role of regional ECCs and ECCV and to table issues that affected the regional Victorian CALD communities.

The ECCV Board nominated me to join the Victoria Eye-Care Service (VES) Advisory Board as their representative. Again, I used that opportunity to table issues of eye-care services access and equity for CALD communities from a regional perspective. I was head-hunted for a position on the Board for Consumer Engagement Council for South East Water, Victoria, where my acquired skills on community engagement were seen as valuable.

I was nominated by the ECCV Board to the Responsible

Gambling Ministerial Advisory Council of Victoria (RGMAC). This Council met three times a year for two hours to discuss State Government's revenue from gambling and the issues of hardships they face because of their addiction. The Mitchell Institute for Education and Health Policy at Victoria University invited me to join their national team to promote and expand the role of self-care in the Australian Health System.

The Asthma Australia's Consumer Advisory Council selected me following an invited interview to be an advocate for the consumers as I had a strong health background.

One other community engagement that linked with my research interests was with the National Health and Medical Research Council of Australia (NHMRC), which is the peak body for research in Australia. I valued my appointed position as a Community Observer and later as the Chairperson for Community Observer Committee on the NHMRC. The aim of the Observer Committee was to provide critical feedback on the adherence by the Assessment Committee on the conflict of interest and confidentiality during the annual week-long, face-to-face meetings in Canberra.

In 2015, I was nominated by ECCV Board to the Victorian Multicultural Commission (VMC). The Minister for Multicultural Affairs, Mr Robyn Scott at the time, appointed me as the Community Representative Commissioner on the Victorian Multicultural Commission because of my valued experience in both academia and wider communities. The conduit role between the state government and communities was very demanding, but the community engagements at those functions were valuable and often very enjoyable. Soon afterwards, in 2020, I was appointed by the Board of the Emotional Well-Being Institute, to be the President for the Institute.

Despite my international appointments, I still continue my work at the local scene. Currently, I still maintain my advisory role with the Hindu communities in Ballarat and support the settlement of new skilled migrants and others who arrive to the region as humanitarian entrants. On reflection, the community invitations to take on senior roles in voluntary organisations increased as I advanced through salaried senior academic positions, and I noticed there was an acknowledgement of skills between voluntary community engagement roles and professional portfolios. I cannot underestimate the similarity between the skills gained during professional positions and those required to hold voluntary senior offices in the community.

‹ **16** ›

The strategy against my hurdles

When I reflect on my life, I am amazed with the things I have done in my 71 years of life. I think of it as amazing because I was born in a very poor environment and struggled to survive. My family hardly had enough to eat during my school days because my dad passed away when I was four years old and my unemployed mother struggled to bring up the six of us. When she left the family home following domestic squabbles, it deprived me of maternal love.

I would not have survived without the support of my siblings. I appreciate the help of my second older sister, Jaya, who welcomed me into her family, despite her own challenging circumstances with three children. I am grateful for the intermittent help of my second brother, Maniam, who was stationed in different parts of the country with his government army role. There were not many happy moments during my childhood days as I was under my oldest brother's tight regime. Despite several traumatic incidents during my stay with my oldest brother, Krish, I cannot thank him enough for his support for my education during my school days.

It was not an easy decision to move away from my country of birth in search of a better future. My brave decision at seventeen was more forward thinking than courage alone. My days labouring to survive in Singapore were not a pleasurable experience. Fortunately, I held on to my hope that one day my difficult times would be over.

My unstoppable passion to continue my education began with the long-awaited remarkable move to Scotland. There, the unexpected, priceless gift I received from the Scottish Government began my high school and university education. Sometimes, I wonder where I would have ended up without those early days of financial support to pursue my career.

On reflection, my earlier education was only denied because of our family's financial hardship, and that made me more determined to seek a University degree. It was only after my undergraduate degree that I valued my own untapped intellectual potential, especially when I received the surprising invitation to do an Honours degree in Zoology from Aberdeen University, together with financial assistance from the Scottish Government. The scholarship from the Queensland Government to complete a Diploma in Nurse Education at QUT furthered my appetite for postgraduate studies. Completing my Masters studies at UNSW, which I managed through nightshift income, was a stressful time but a remarkable achievement.

My final thirst for education was whetted when I completed my PhD studies at Melbourne University, and it was a most delightful moment when my doctoral thesis was passed with no corrections!

My professional career path was equally successful through my continuous hard work. I am amazed with myself on how a person like me from a poverty stricken background was able to reach a professorial level in a competitive academic world.

In my desperate days in Singapore, I only wished for a clerical position, but my strenuous labouring experience made me dream beyond being a clerk. When I completed my nursing in Dundee, pursuing my education beyond nursing became more than a dream. It was the position as a Nurse Educator at the School of Nursing at Princess Alexandra Hospital that paved my confidence to further my career in academia. I ambitiously made up my mind to become a university lecturer, which motivated me to finish my Masters at UNSW and also began the preparation for academic life. Following the appointment as a lecturer at the University of Ballarat, I began to ask the question, 'What is next?'

My progression to the position of Senior Lecturer in the Rural Clinical School at the University of Melbourne gave me the confidence to reach further, so when the three-year appointment at Melbourne University ended, I was not perturbed, but decided to try harder. Again, not long afterwards, I secured a position as an Associate Professor in the School of Medicine at James Cook University. After my three years of academic work, I resigned my position from James Cook, but not long after I was appointed as a Professor with the Emotional Well-Being Institute in Geneva.

On reflection, I realise that I have been very fortunate and my career has surpassed beyond my dreams. Of course, I had a track record of working hard as a pre-requisite to gain those required essential qualifications and publications to prove my credentials, which were mandatory in pursuing academic career advancement. From a position as a lecturer to the level of professor was a big achievement for me!

My journey has been successful with God's blessing and my family is equally happy. My wife, who enjoyed her full-time senior position at the local hospital, finally decided to retire to spend more time with our granddaughter, Amira who is growing up in San Francisco where my daughter, Anuja and son-in-law, Ashley work. My son, while managing his own engineering company, also completed his PhD in Wireless Engineering from Melbourne University. As the family is busy, I continue my engagements with the diverse communities in official and unofficial capacities at local, national and international levels.

When I reflect how my humble beginnings led me to positions of influence where I was able to make significant changes, I found it related to the few key strategies I applied along the way.

- *Firstly, have a mind to change the situation or move away from the situation*
  In my case I was in a situation (after my studies in Malaysia) where nothing was going to change for me unless I did something radical. When I was 17 years old, unfortunately, I was in no position to do anything because I had no money or people who could help

me in my desperate situation. The only option was to move away from the very distressing situation I was in because I could not change my situation by remaining there. That was the time when I set my mind to move from Malaysia to Singapore.

- **Do not hesitate to take action to explore any glimpse of hope or possible opportunities**
  As my situation was desperate with no job to survive or study, I never hesitated to take the initiative to explore what could be out there. At that time, I had heard that young people who went to Singapore immediately found jobs. I did not even know the details of job opportunities. I did not know the kind of jobs offered, the wages, accommodation support, company culture and the safety standards or work permit assistance for migrant workers from Malaysia. It was a big gamble!

  The only message I had was that the Malaysian migrant teenagers were readily employed in labouring positions had given me the smallest glimpse of hope to leave for Singapore.

  At that time, it is very daunting to try something that I had not done before; that is, to leave the country. I too had all the thoughts about things that could go wrong, but I was at the bottom of the pit in my life and nothing could make it worse at that time!

- **Remain resilient during moments of despair**
  It was very difficult for me to maintain a positive mind

when things were not going my way, or the people I knew were not supportive. So, it was the hardest thing at that time to remain calm and at the same time I wanted to kill myself.

Even in my school-going age, I craved for parental love, but my family circumstances denied that opportunity for me. I remembered the depressing days when I walked in the heat and sun, in Singapore, looking for a factory labourer's job. Even in Australia, following my university education and after six months of job attempts, I only secured a temporary newspaper delivery work. In those examples of situations, to remain positive and calm with hope will not be an easy task for anyone. My sorrowful situations were shared with my guardian, Lord Ganesha, who gave me the strength and positivity to not give up my journey.

- *Gain any available experience while waiting for the ideal job*

While I was seeking the position that suited my experience and qualifications, I had several earlier jobs which I embraced. In Singapore, after my School Certificate qualification, I worked as a labourer, while several Singapore citizens with similar qualifications had secured administrative positions. During my university vacation, I accepted work as a hospital porter. After my undergraduate degree, I was only able to find a job as an insurance agent, which generally does not need any qualification above secondary school level.

Several of those jobs were very junior to my level of qualification at that time, but they never failed to teach me something. Despite the low incomes from those jobs, I found my interpersonal skills had improved. I gained knowledge about how companies and organisations operate and understood how their hierarchy systems were structured.

- *Be actively innovative to improve your skills and knowledge*

  Initially, when I applied for senior positions in the university sector, I was often not short-listed because I did not have the leadership skills. Unfortunately, I could not gain those skills, prior to applying because I was not in a senior position.

  My community engagement interest offered me the opportunity to develop my leadership skills, which were very evident when I formed the Ballarat Regional Multicultural Council, the peak body for ethnic communities in the region. Soon after, senior appointees at university levels not only acknowledged my leadership skills but also my contribution to the community. It was no surprise when I was invited to be on several boards because of my academic seniority and community experience.

- *Celebrate the moments of every achievement*

  In my life, till I resigned from full-time position, there were continuous hurdles along the way that I had to

overcome to reach my goal. I did not fail to acknowledge and celebrate all my achievements, despite some of them being very small. For example, I celebrated when I got a job as a labourer in Singapore. Often the positive energy from the celebration at that moment was sufficient enough to keep me going until I successfully cleared the next hurdle.

- *Enjoy the moments in giving*

  In my life, I undoubtedly had received help from my family in my childhood. Without their help I would not have survived or completed my secondary education. I am grateful for the undergraduate education support from the Scottish Government. The valuable help from friends and the community cannot be denied.

  Currently, I reflect on that help and feel very fortunate to be able to help others to reach their potential. I am able to provide some financial help to my siblings and families who had helped me in the past. I enjoy my moments of voluntary work at local, state, national and international levels. Each of these voluntary contributions bring me joy and satisfaction which I hope to continue and enjoy the moments of giving.

  These few strategies mentioned above have helped me, and I hope they may be of help to you too.

www.ingramcontent.com/pod-product-compliance
Lightning Source LLC
Chambersburg PA
CBHW021141080526
44588CB00008B/159